MORE POEMS FOR PEOPLE

To Dorothy Livesay

with grateful thanks for her permission to incorporate the title of her book "Poems for People" in the title of this book.

(Dorothy Livesay began in this book in the tradition of Canadian poets who dedicated their poems and their lives to the working class.)

Also by Milton Acorn

In Love and Anger (1956)
Against a League of Liars (1960)
The Brain's the Target (1960)
Jawbreakers (1963)
A special edition of "Fiddlehead" entitled 58 Poems by Milton Acorn (1963)
I've Tasted My Blood (1969)
several anthologies

MORE
POEMS
FOR PEOPLE

MILTON ACORN

NC PRESS 1972

Cover Portrait by Greg Curnoe.

Revised Edition 1973

Acorn, Milton,
More Poems for People
819.1
ISBN—0-919600-01-8

New Canada Publications, a division of
NC Press Ltd.
Box 6106, Terminal A,
Toronto 1, Ontario.

PRINTED IN CANADA BY UNION LABOUR

MILTON

MARCH 6/72

CONTENTS

Bethuniverse

Does a man three decades dead walk and make facial expressions
Among us? When we're shaving do our eyes stray from
    the mirror
And suddenly in vision's discarded corner
Do we see his face? Surely there's a reasonable explanation . . .

A strong old man gets on the elevator. He
Even has a red sweatshirt — tam tilted at that old angle.
If I could see his eyes I'd know;
But his eyes are screwed shut
                  as if in anguish:

Like many eyes   —   opening, closing   —   record anguish . . .
One sees him again; in many sizes; at many ages;
Suddenly I realize there are many Bethunes.
From many candidates, fate chooses
Both its victims and its heroes
Often one and the same . . .
Another necessity, another Canuck, and there could have
    been another Bethune.

So many of us live in anguish
Because we were spared his anguish . . .

Let there be a Bethune Oath
Improving on that of Hippocrates
To make curing no routine but wars against disease;
Strengthen health, increase and lead it
Into all which must be done, all which must be felt, meant
    and seen.

What are we doing? Brave Canucks :
After four hundred years still a colony?
Supplying the basic armstuffs
To conquer a world which includes us?
Since one of us swerved time from its course
There's been no rest.
                Why call it peace?

(version 11-3-73)

9

Live with me on Earth

Live with me on Earth among red berries and the bluebirds
And leafy young twigs whispering
Within such little spaces, between such floors of green,
    such figures in the clouds
That we could want and win, want and win, win and want
    again.

Where the stars past the spruce copse mingle with the fireflies
Or the dayscape flings a thousand tones of light back at the sun —
Be any one of the colors of an Earth lover;
Walk with me and sometimes cover your shadow with mine.

Live with me on Earth under the invisible daylight Moon,
Both her face and her shadow gone but she still there.
Tide-rise : tide-fall; every wave and molecule has a lean in
    her direction :
Where thoughts and actions appropriate to a man

Rise amid the welter of winter storms
    — the storms of his words, the grey nul-calm
                of his winter mind —
Where the pages of a book by Irving Layton
Or any other poet who has forgotten
Flutter   —   unlike a butterfly tethered with a thread.

Where, like changing letters in a fluid script
The southerning songbird flocks ride swift, slide
And skate they seem to do rather than fly over a picture-scape
    glissant as ice.
Up they rise, down they go, til from their eyesview

The horizon's rocking : whether it's hill or plain
Mountain range, squirm ruffle or shadow-calm of the sea;
Over all this the songflocks sail like shifting letters
Til you think they're signaling indefinite things to you,
                definite things to other birds.

Live with me on Earth where so many signals are flown
Some in distress, some meant to cause distress;
Learn the distinguishment of which to answer, which to blast
Til the song of Earth's survival shall incorporate our voices.

Live with me on Earth among the songs of orioles,
        squirrels singing sometimes like birds,among crickets
And frogs singing sometimes like crickets,
        sometimes like bull-calves,
Sometimes like frogs. Live with me on Earth
Where green is a theme of the land,
        varying and contrasting with all colours :

Where a word, a sentence, a philosophy
Expands and regathers itself; like a nude athlete
Flings oneself's fatigued body
Onto the grassy bank while the crowd's yell grows dim —

And if this or that does not rise, someone will rise
When a thought leaps and skips like the recorded note of a bugle
Stored and then replayed, leaps and skips
Gathering newness from each listener.

17-12-71

Rabbie Still Be With Us

Canucks wha hae bled beside Mackenzie
    — last man to retreat from Montgomery's Tavern
    — haven't we got a Scottish situation?
Much more in common than good whiskey.

Except that as itself, Canada never was free
The name meaning 'a collection of huts'
Absent from Europe's loot-begotten splendour
Indians noticed this and pitied us.

It not being there were no ships
Or Indians never sailed on them;
They recognized us first as slaves
Black and/or White in a broken chain of nigger-cabins.

Like a Rosary snapped in the pocket
To which a calloused palsied arthritic hand still reaches;
As a miner still pans for stray nuggets
Breathing painfully in a vision of wealth,

Or a poker-player clutches his tenth mediocre hand
Hoping for a deviation of odds
While the bland owner of the casino
Walks by in a checkered vest, smoking a royal cigar.

And like pimples on the land huts spread
Their approach heralded and cleared by the small-pox;
Buffalo disappeared, replaced by oxen
Who respected fences   —   lay still for the branding iron.

All this we propagated, even tho it never suited us,
From MacLauchlin to Bisset our poets protested;
Less a passion than an habitual religion
We spoke loyally of Free Enterprise —
      even while it was sickening us.

We did nothing we couldn't have done without it
Which was the creed of another country
Whose inhabitants differed from us
In that no matter what they gained, they never thought
                                  they had enough.

"There'll always be an England as long as Scotland's there"
And always a U.S.A. so long as Canada's friendly;
The trouble being the Yanks have no friends, only suckers :
Can any nation live with such external cares?

MacKenzie never thought of help from the Ojibway,
There all the time   —   just waiting to be asked;
Who came in hundreds to see Lount hang
Doing him honor, wellmixed with irony.

So Riel talked with God? Well so did his mother
Who was Indian. Indians had always talked with God.
His bible-thumping captors, when it came to money matters
Thought a man who consulted God was crazy.

To think of Dumont, the ever-victorious general
Seeing the defences of Batoche; saying
"Here you'll witness my first defeat"
His genius, estimation hadn't left him.

The noblest, bravest, most farseeing of us
Have found themselves tributary to lesser men
Like Bethune retreating first to Spain, then China
To shake the whole world : finally even Canada;

Or our second MacLauchlin, Big Jim fleeing to death from
        Tim Buck's orders.
If God's out of the picture blame that Cape Bretoner
For you can be sure he harried Hell :
With the Devil gone what work is left for God?

Our tears forbidden along with our history
If allowed to flow could fill a line of hogsheads
For all of us to click our glasses over
And drink with the Scots *to the king across the water.*

Not to a king. Not us : *To The People Across The Water.*
Let the record of their freedom be our memory
So the wild cries of pipes ring out
To a folk which once was free. Shall be — and so will we.

They were never defeated. And neither were we.
Their leaders were bought — ours sold from the first.
On a hundred foreign fields crosses and shattered corpses
Commemorate our pointless victories.

A spell both ancestors and descendents'ld marvel at
    — the spell of bourgeoisdom made us fritter away
Our chances for freedom. Now in this age tormented
Like a planet beset by comets, when the bourgeoisie's

Twisting on its seat of crime; let's help hustle them
Off the world. In the face of Empires and
Their pompous Liberals, their bullying experts,
Make sure the People rule here — Ourselves our own way.

28/7/72

Riding with Joe Hensby

Riding with Joe Hensby in a ten-speed trailer
Down 401 the cab so high we're on a flying throne;
No need to worry of traffic, it worries of you . . .
The jungle trails clear when the elephant comes.

Thirty tons of steel behind, fifty miles an hour :
No need to worry — if we got stopped sudden
And all that metal came crashing through
You could spread us on a sandwich and we'd never know.

He plays the gears like a man at a piano
Cursing every time — two or three seconds apart;
At no one in particular
He lives the road . . . he lives the abstract world of his curses.
Sometimes I come into his consciousness, but no one else.

But when that stream of vehicles clogs, we slow :
    sitting up there like conjoint kings
One of us's got to point a moral; and I
The official poet : —
                        "Jesus Christ Joe
There's ten million dollars of equipment in sight
    — how is it that we're poor?"

Call it a machine, call it a beast, call it a kind of a hand
For it becomes an extension of the man.
When it roars it's we together are the lion :
And we live like lions
                        often moving, often waiting
                        years to pounce.

15-6-71

Poem on Life Insurance and Combat Aviation

'We relish dogfights among ourselves'
Say The Life Insurance Companies In Canada
: and above this print a full-page picture
of Tommies and Jerries (First World War)
(so campy and comforting to think most of 'em'd be dead now
                              anyway)
in combat under a cloud
(to represent I suppose the threat of nationalization
    — if the cloud were bigger there'd be no combat)
'Which may come as a surprise to people'
                    it says
                    there
                    definitely not
                    here
'who thinks the life insurance industry [sic] is some
kind of club.
Every life insurance company in Canada
is distinctly independent'
                    (so are the two halves of a siamese twin

                    the question is
                    how *distinctly*
'If you look closely you'll be amazed
how unlike we are.
We offer different policies, different prices
different services, different philosophies [*oh migod; sic*]
We're not dismayed by those differences
We prize them. They keep our business
contemporary, our products low in cost [sic 'em boy].

In fact we're rather proud that as an
industry, we seldom totally agree on anything'
          (except   —   italics and brackets
                    mine
                    mine
                    mine
          the discouragement of life insurance councillors)
'These ads we've been running (this is the
last of the current series)'
                    (in fact it's the first and only)
                    (Maaaaaaaaaaaaaa M.A.)
(but since I'm almost the only person
to read the papers thuroly —
                    that makes me almost the only one
                    not to be grabbed by the scalp of guilt
                    when I read this indigo lie)
And in the picture of the dogfight
There's a mighty irregular curve of smoke-like printer's ink,
                    expanding towards its furthest end,
To represent I'm supposed to assume
A life insurance company going down in flames
With employees, policy-holders and investors aboard
(or perhaps it's meant to represent
the Ontario Medicare plan going down in flames
from too much credulence given to
                    nonsense like this . . .)
'But that's the way it goes sometimes
In a free [sick] economy.'
                    says the ad
Which, I repeat
     is
     by
The Life Insurance Companies In Canada
                    not 'Of Canada'
                    or even 'Canadian'

At Dawson Creek Hotel

Like single rocks from space hitting the moon
The fist of the Québéçois in the next room
Thump . . . Thump . . . Thump . . . Far into the night
                — I make no objection
The turbulence of his mind matches the turbulence of mine.

In the daytime he has visitors. Thru the wall
I can't make out much except his larynx grating again and again
"C'est pa'd' juste . . . C'est pa'd' juste!" *

The town's afflicted with workless wanderers.
Indian and White . . . Native and foreign
They came in honesty, came with honor;
Came to labour: And there is none.

This town afflicts the workless wanderers
(c'est pa'd' juste — c'est pa'd' juste)
Too much to care for, to care for without purpose
(c'est pa'd' juste — c'est pa'd' juste)

Late into the night I hear his fist. Late into the day
I hear his voice as if it was grinding rock.
"C'est pa'd' juste . . . C'est pa'd' juste!"

"This is not justice . . ."

1969-71

18

Red and the Mountain

Like a shawl thrown over a woman's shoulders
The narrow cloud trailed along the mountain
And there was me, shouting to Red Lane
"Get it Red! Get the ITNESS of it!"

I'd studied that mountain for three years
And studied many similar clouds
And nothing had impressed me so much
That the poem is not the thing;
So high and yet its counters so smooth
And clouds like that so appropriate to it.

And I never knew a man who in his own presence
That the thought of him was so close to what he was
(perhaps I saw him, even then, as I see him now
    — the absoluteness of death
                        cast on a thin screen of life)
Perhaps I was begging him to write the poem I couldn't
The poem of the mountain which would be the mountain.

I never knew a man who so combined
Consent and refusal. In him they were one and the same.
The mountain's still there and Red's dead;
But what'll it be in ten million years time?
The hills are dissolving like sugar candy,
The process slower, but no less certain.

What will Red Lane be then?
                    Still part of the rocks
    — an undiscovered fossil.

29-5-71

What Right has He . . . ?

What right has he to grow hair to his hips
As if he belonged to a different century?
I know him and his friends claim he washes it :
But don't believe it   —   Who could spare the time?

These are different times . . . Everybody's got to be the same.
I do my job . . . I know I'm not the best
But the best men don't get ahead anyway
Except by too much effort   —   Medium is wisest.

And he's got the nerve to say my job's useless,
Only a lot of bureaucratic bungling;
Managing welfare   —   keeping half myself . . .
Well haven't I got the right? Ain't I working?

What right has he to have such a long penis?
It's damned indecent   —   hanging to his knees!
And that sneaky way he has of hiding it!
Telling his woman not to brag . . . Damn' foreigner I'd say!

What right has he to walk up and down the street
Swinging his head by the hair like a lunchpail?
I know he claims modern science makes it possible :
But what about probable? Imitators might fail.

In his last incarnation I'm told
He wouldn't cut his tail like a proper spaniel :
Gave himself backaches trying to stand up human-fashion.
"I can talk! I can talk!" he contended . . .
His accent was bad . . . Just like barking . . .
Most people thought the whole effort terrible.

And once before (he'll tell you) he was a woman
But wouldn't act like it. She governed an empire
And did it well   —   Only for a while though.
Men of good will ganged up and set her on fire.

What right has he, I ask, to jump out of his skin
And send his stuffed hide to important social functions?
He says the dummy enjoys it and he doesn't . . .
What if everybody did that? (maybe they do)

Everyone can see he belongs to no proper race —
So covered with birthmarks he's practically piebald . . .
Still he goes round with an impudent grin on his face
Less like a man than some ape out of place.

And all in all, what right has he to complain?
Hasn't he got   —   by sheer nerve and ability
A good position? Says he doesn't like
People being unhappy . . . Hell, he makes them unhappy!

I knew a man who got ordered by a judge
To tell all the poor people to go to hell :
He couldn't do it   —   poor too long himself —
Told the judge to go to hell and went to jail . . .

I met him in the Presidential Palace
Where he'd allow landscapes, abstracts, but no mirrors
(not in the palace actually, in the gardener's cottage)
There were too many portraits of him in that country.

1967-71

I'll be a Statue to Myself

I'll be a statue to myself. Cigar stuck out
Like the smooth broken-off stump of a dead limb
Burning to maintain the chemical balance
As much part of me as a chimney
Symbolizing (what the hell does it symbolize?)

I'll walk like a statue, the earth my plinth.
Head up, and whether it's joy, gloom passing for sorrow,
A tiger grin willed me by an Indian,
Snarl of triumph, snarl in rebuke of defeat
Which guarantees its cancellation. Head up
Usually but sometimes head down
It'll always express one thing . . . determination
Usually determination about some thing I know
But sometimes just determination   —   something'll
        come along to be determined about.

Yes, I symbolize something. Yes, the cigar does.
I symbolize an old depression workman, jokes all the
        time, jokes loaded with hate;
And the cigar . . . That's the Capitalist's cigar
Taken by me to indicate I'm going to take much more.
That thing happened. I saw. It's not going to be forgotten.
I see it happen again, every day in smaller doses.
No repentance . . . No forgiveness. That's God's rule
        and mine.
(like Lenin I've never wavered : the misfortune of this
        country
is the resemblance between me and Lenin ends there.)

I'll be a statue to myself. Except now and again
Someone remembers I am no statue;
When I'm permitted to make a joke
Without explaining its profound significance.
Women too, odd ones and ones of them,
Sometimes realize I am no statue . . .
Then I cease to be what I am.
Blood boils like maple syrup. Semen flows. I write
          love poems.

I'll be a statue to myself. Never raise one while I live.
I change (as a matter of fact bronze changes too)
And tho you look at me again to say, "No change,"
The fact is I'm changing, in a different dimension
Which always seems the same to you.

I'll be a statue to myself. While I live let that suffice.
But if I die (for which I have no plans)
You can raise one more if you like
Of bronze, granite, carborundum, diamond or ice.
Don't forget the cigar. Keep it burning
Preferably as a beacon for mariners :
As for that number two statue   —   make it hollow.
Put a little doll inside, gyrating thru motions, poses,
          shapes like every version of the question mark
          in every script.
That'll be me at my real age . . . Nine years.

25-27/6/71

Soliloquy in Billiard Balls

The poet's mindseye (twinned and more than twinned
like those of a woman about to give birth
   — multiple births, at least multiple eventually;
or like twin suns (space is speckled like great dice
. . . at one moment throwing out flamelike prominences
the next moment quiet (tho these moments
     don't correspond either;
juggling their planets, changing them with their
     curious lights and tides

This eye   —   it's neither like the inventor's, some politicians'
Tho it too casts its colours on time
Even as sudden; tho oftener
The brush which is the out going view
Is a slower thing   —   redipping itself darker and darker.

(the critic's false teeth, or the false critic's teeth
begin to take on the shape of a sneer, like
some phenomena beyond Saturn
more beautiful far than a critic . . .
I've gone and written an abstract line; I've plagiarized
     Shakespeare
   — tho those planets are undoubtedly there —
I've written in argument, tho Shakespeare undoubtedly
     wrote in argument;
I've written my own argument   —   not the critic's
argument, immutable, unchangedly true it is assumed
since before lightbulbs began
and the suns too (applied without qualm to everything,
     tho never stated . . .

It (the poet's eye — not previously named and
      obnoxious things)
Doesn't always start from his physical and electrical
Presence or anywhere he is by usual definition :
It can start from a past as sure or surer
Than printed in any volume;
A past partly or entirely imagined,
Some place which never existed but could, or else couldn't;
Or some future, some imagined future
Without which a man is no more complete
Than he is without hands or sperm . . .

                    (thinking about it for maybe two
                    months . . . maybe months longer)

It's the Last Stormtime

It's the last stormtime of winter. As if the ghosts of
                              ancestors
Forgetting even they are ancestors
Were wandering. They cannot groan so the trees groan
                              for them;
The hiss of the snows is their wordless breath.

Survivors they were who hunted survivors
The stumbling moose, the slumbering bear, the rabbit . . .
Always winter was the season of their wanderings
And now they wander like fragmented crystals of snow.

It's the last stormtime, when summer seems a fantasy,
Something dreamt of, a visit to another planet.
Gawd I feel I was an oversize dumptruck
Loaded with everything that fell this year;
All the snow, all the soot and debris in it.

Somewhere else, in space both and time,
The snow's cleaner, but no less fierce.
Now when even the dullest eye looks up for the faintest
                              hint or hope of blue;
When it's unthinkable that winter once was pleasant;
Now's the thing like a moment when somewhere, somewhen
The ancestors are wandering; cold, hunger, tiredness,
The void in the head where there should be memory — all
                              these are the same.

They must slay the great beast of spring
Whose decay is a field of berries, whose decay is
                    the oneeyed sun
In whose yellow lashes all colors revive
And the living remember who they were
So the dead perhaps may remember too.

Already It Seems You Haunt this Cottage

Already it seems you haunt this cottage
Tho you've never been here, have promised to come.
Oh Rose, there are thousands of waves in the bay
And every one spells 'welcome'.

When I met you first I thought you were Scots
And I've got a weakness for Scottish girls;
Though 'weakness' seems the wrong word.
Oughtn't it, instead, be 'strength'.

                    first said in a letter

They've Murdered Two Workers

They've murdered two workers in Sept-Iles.
Who was they? A Chevrolet
Courtesy of General Motors :
Biggest part of the American Empire.

They've murdered two workers in Sept-Iles
Where I was treated better than anyplace else in my life.
If you say we *anglais* should stick together;
I was fired from the Iron Ore Company
Fair-square as *anglais* as
a computer set on the shoulderblades
Of a mannikin to use for a head

Or a head packed with bourgeois thoughts
Set on the shoulders of a worker
For somebody drove that car
And he was *Québécois.*

   It's one step from 'I'm guilty — we're all guilty'
to 'he's guilty' *or* 'they're guilty' : *considering guilt
as a general thing . . . Not particular, like the man who
drove the car.*
      *To say I was fired implies guilt to some,
when actually it was because I knew more than the foreman*
         . . . or maybe just the signal-look
         I sent ahead of me into eyes
         was recognized.

      Wandering around Sept-Iles
With seven cents in my pocket
Down the other side of the street
Came an Acadian I knew,
And within an hour I had

                              a job
                              a place to eat
                              and a place to sleep
It wasn't so much a company
As a co-operative gang of carpenters,
One of whom knew more than the rest
So he was foreman,
One of whom had a quick tongue
So he negotiated with the boss
Who turned up once a week with the paychecks.

That's the way it was then.
It differs today.

After praising all my merits
The Acadian (Gerry LeBlanc) said
There's just one thing wrong with this man
He can't speak French.
                    The foreman (six-foot-six
                    in a voice very deep) asked
"Es'q'il parle le bois?"
                    Does he speak wood.

They've murdered two workers in Sept-Iles
Where I was treated better than anyplace in my life.
After three months I got lonesome for the sound
                    of my own language.
Who wouldn't? Ask any Québéçois . . .

The Acadian had a daughter
Who when I was leaving was about to get married
So for all I know
One of the workers killed
Or one of the thirty injured
Was his grandson.

No doubt they had a funeral
And no doubt at some point the priest said
"We are all guilty . . ." which I consider a damned lie.

If there's no Heaven;
And especially if there is no Hell;
That proves there's no God.

25/5/72

Again Sept-Iles

I shall donate my heart to science.
It's 49 years old, but I'll swear it's still serviceable
And maybe the doctors will get a shock
If on that heart they find a tatoo
Which reads "Sept-Iles"

The workers there said *"en greve"*
Which in Canada I suppose means "On Strike"
But I suspect
That in Québec
It would more correctly read
"No Fooling Around!"

They took over the radio station
Which is probably the reason we know anything
      about it at all.

25/5/72

To Rose

The time's come round again, and you are time.
The days go by, some bright some cloudy
The nights go by, some dark some starry.
You are the day. You are the night.

I can't stop thinking of our two bodies;
What fantastic differences! Strange too
That this, on me, is part of you;
And this, in you, is part of me.

I love you like the old carven stones
I pick up on this beach   —   and the bones you pick up.
They're the very tools my ancestors held in their hands;
And what if you should pick up a strange bone?

The Dolphin Knight

The dolphin knight, elected king for a day
Or ace, jack, joker, humble and/or mysterious blank
Or wild deuce — wherever he's settled in the shuffle
Or throw of dice . . . Analogy doesn't suffice
To portray just one part of the game in which
        the fine stroke of play
Is the appointed one's discovery of what he really is
        because he really wants . . .

(the ocean's hung with and crossed by schools as a sky is
        with clouds,
individual fish breaking off like rain
though what we'd call a sky is definite as if honed —
indeed the sky, our kind of sky's in the downward direction
always a night, a pit in which dim stars wander . . .
but darkness is not the same to a dolphin
as it is to a sighted man, perhaps more like a blind man's . . .
he calls, continuously and repeatedly, something,
        maybe his name
and everything in range calls its name back at him)

And the dolphin does, or some thing does, or something
        will do
Not only discover maps with his voice, but construct them :
It is like a paradise with many kinds of chess castles
Plus other things more marvelous (we can't yet imagine) . . .
It is a world, a play with himself the entire cast
The dolphin knight, elected for this, throws out
        for his entire clan
To move through, questioning, arguing in gracious Spanish,
        crying defiance like opera singers . . .

(how do you bring the women in, describing like this?
Is a dolphin male a man? A female a woman?
Functions are functions, but outside of that
You might as well call them a third and fourth sex of Man . . .
Unless we too, overlaid by our functions
have in disguise many sexes   —   apparent now only
        as perversions
(and where's the perversion? in the person
or in things static and moving, constructions of Humanity?)
The world is full of cries and echoes, ours no less
        than the Dolphins :
Our hands know the world, can hardly know without
        changing it
(A matter of degree, but the degree's large, qualitative)

Would not one who changed less finally   —   dare more?
It's a matter of becoming accustomed to change
And changing as we wish, not in the darks of wishless engines;
Who, creatures of perverted wishes   —   often perverted
        wishes
Give rise in turn to more perverted wishes
Til the balls manipulate the juggler, the engine
        cuts off the human head;
Sets it on itself to operate without human juices . . .

                                                                Altho

This is actually an analogy :
The body simply fades, becomes of little account
And the head of the machine man, in turn
Is reproduced in countless duplicates
To set, complete with thoughts, upon the necks
        of his countless slaves.

But isn't this a matter of degree? You and I
Don't our brains — their parts wave like seaweed —
    sparkle with energy
In conversation, work, play, all deeds of ecstacy?
And are not matter and energy the same?
Does not your word gathered in the energies of your brain
Make a little shift to become your voice
Another little one to become what I hear, to become
    what whirls in my brain
And what I answer — isn't that part of yourself thrown
    back at you
Out of part of yourself? Are not we two one?
Ourselves an analogy for Humanity?

The Dolphin knight, elected king for a day
Or for whatever role in which he is still king
Lives whole lives, entire lifetimes
In a world that's all his til the next celebration
When he comes into another's world, knows the whole
    content of another's life :
Thus all are one because each one is one
As a strangeness but not a stranger; not as a Human
    stuck up like a bowling pin.
If we could be that, so of each other, for each other;
Willing to let another's thoughts be blood
And drip into our nerves as into veins
Would there be any end to us, in space or time?

27/6/71

In Ottawa Streets

In Ottawa's streets the civil servants
on the way to work, travel in flocks   —   pedestrian
yet somehow giving an impression like flying
as if each individually was trying to give an impression
        of flying
though hardly the impression one does give   —   like spray.

If I were to name the bird, I'd pick the Lesser Blue Heron
for fat civil servants are rare, upper-echelon, and not
        of this poem.
Their suits were once good. Once every decade or decade
        and a half
when one of them buys a suit; it's good : prestige demands this
: and when it comes the time for patches
On knee or elbow; they're sewn there carefully to give
        the impression
that they were always meant to be there. Invisible mending
also thrives in Ottawa. Still
patches are to be seen in the oddest places,
and yet the tailors (or the boys' wives)
have developed such skill this too seems to be part
        of the design.

The archaic smile   —   known from ancientest Greek
        statuary
is very close to the expression of an Ottawa civil servant
except, upon the Rideau . . . the teeth show
which gives (head going back and forth like a weathercock
        in a shifting wind)
an impression of dash. In some metaphysical way
        they're going somewhere;
tho as actual, physical parts of this earth (a fact
        their whole stance tries to deny)
they're souls on the way to limbo, caught in a headwind,
        doomed never to get there

Hey You Guevara

Hey You Guevara!
It isn't fit at a Communist funeral
To say there will be none nobler than you —
There shall be nobler, as you if you had lived, would
      have become nobler
As nobility will become the property of any person,
Born into or soon learned,
As nobility will become a simple reflex
Buried among emotions which will be nobler still
And for which today we have no names . . .

Hey You Guevara!
Neither is it fit at the grave of a Communist
To say his loss will ever be redeemed
For we Communists curse death as we curse the bourgeois
      ministers of death   —
Count none of our own, none of the oppressed or
      fighters for the oppressed
Ever replaceable, that your death-wound or the
    death-wound of an unknown baby who'll die
      next week
Who would have lived if you had lived
Will ever stop bleeding.

The Cuban Revolutionaries had two great leaders
One called 'Fidel' (faithful)
And one called 'Ernesto' (earnest)
It proved to be too much for the Cuban Revolutionaries
To have two leaders called 'Faithful' and 'Earnest'
So they nick-named the other one 'Che' (Hey)
Which I've interpreted in the sense of "Hey You"
(and if I've made a joke at a Communist funeral
be assured that Che, if he could be here would make one too)

36

Hey You Guevara !
It's entirely appropriate at a Communist funeral
To salt one's praise with criticism, if criticism is what's due . . .
Hey You Guevara! Hey You damn fool
Guevara you've made a liar of me
Who once when you were rumoured dead and the rumour was untrue
And I knew it was untrue   —   didn't figure:
I wrote a poem called "Where is Che Guevara?"
Describing you alive —
                              True enough then:
Describing you behaving as a Marxist-Leninist
Which wasn't true. You met your death doing a piece
    of non-Bolshevik stupidity.
Hey You Guevara! Hey You damn fool:
How could you go into an alien country wielding
    Your reputation like a club
Demanding to be made Commander there?
How could you not bother even to learn what language was
    spoken there;
Try to arouse the peasants in Spanish
When you might as well caw like a crow?
How dared you then call these unmoved people rocks?
I don't speak Spanish either
And assure you I'm no rock . . .

Hey You Guevara!
It's almost trite at the grave of a Communist
To say you are not dead, that you continue to live in us —
For you have breathed so often, there are so many molecules
    in the wind and the winds are so wide
That right this moment your breath's in our lungs
Is in our blood, is in the muscles about our heart-valves —
It's that you've thought such thoughts that they're ours,
Have raged such rages that they're ours,
                              have loved such loves;
Have done such deeds that the confidence of their
    memory is part of the strength
                              of our wills . . .

Hey You Guevara!
I read this poem   — the first version of this poem   —
        in the hall of a Canadian Union :
Where being a clown even when I intended not to be
I said :
                "Some of you are here because you're Communists
                Some are not here because they're Communists
                Some of you are here because you're curious
                        — a natural Human quality
                Which I welcome : and some here because
                        you're not Communists but sympathize :
                Nevertheless I greet you all!"
Yes, I said "Some are not here because you're Communists!"
And there were chuckles in the room
Because The Communist Party of Glorious Memory of Canada
Was holding a meeting on the floor above
To decide whether or whether not to attend
As if a man has to hold a solemn debate over the body
        of a dead tiger.
By the time they decided to come the meeting was over

Hey You Guevara!
I said I read this poem in a hall in Canada
Whose two most known exports are wheat and
physical courage :
Therefore knowing courage we honour courage
Although it never did us much good
                                until now

Hey You Guevara!
Let no man woman or child Communist here resolve
        on his or her own death,
        on your death again in us   —
Tho we'll face that, choose and walk right into it if it be for life,
        for your life and the lives of all who accept life   —
All that life means, the conceivable and as yet
        unconceivable . . .
We'll tell stories of you, true and also legends

But

Hey You Guevara! What about your enemies!?
What'll we tell our children about your enemies?
In times that'll come? In times when they'll no longer exist?
How'll we explain those enemies were Human?
When no such type of Human as they are will be known?
As we invented Santa Claus, God and the Devil
We'll have   —   for the sake of children's stories   —
          to invent some other
          enemies,
          Dragons perhaps, or
                    Vampires
To later explain those Dragons, Vampires;
Were Bourgeois, Imperialist
And Human . . .
                    A sort of Human no longer known.

(I want no applause
Unless it be silent, for yourselves;
Then only if you can accept where your heartsblood
          races through your brains
That you are Guevara)

Hey
     YOU
          Guevara
               ! ?

My heart's a kicking embryo
Where all who live, lived, or might have lived
Grow questioning everything but life . . .
I do not believe Guevara's death
Or anyone elses, or my own

39

Proposed Dedication for a Monument to
Lount and Matthews

This plaque was erected to the memory
of Samuel Lount, a blacksmith but not a simple one . . . who on
April 12th, 1838 was hanged here by ruthless imperialists
bureaucrats and class tyrants, for doing the best deed of his life
fighting for the freedom of his nation, Canada, and of the
      working people : a freedom still unobtained

This man died for liberty
There is no need to fear his fate
He'd still, if he'd stayed wakeful late
Be sleeping these times any way.

This plaque is also dedicated to the memory
of Peter Matthews, farmer, not simple either;
who at this same place, King and Toronto Streets,
      Toronto, Ontario, Canada,
on the same day, at the same time of day
was legally murdered along with Lount
for committing the same rightful action.

Let those whose tribute to the powers they fear
Consists of a hopeless sigh, an sardonic jeer,
Know that freedom is the breath of the mind;

      More to be desired

Than hearing to the deaf, sight to the blind;
A surer way of movement to the lame,
Without freedom, no one really has a name.

The Garbageman is Drunk

The garbageman is drunk. He's on a toot. For seven years he worked on the garbage. Actually he's not the garbageman proper; he's not a driver so he's never been promoted — so actually he's a helper. His correct title would be 'Garbageman's Helper': his help consisting of doing most of the work. But you should be polite and call him 'the garbageman'. After all, anybody who'd been to sea for seven years would properly be called 'a seaman'; even if he was only the cabinboy. Actually I'd never realized he'd been on the job for seven years — longer than most cats, for instance, live: so you could with justice call it a lifetime. But neither me or anyone else I know of except him had realized it was seven years. Time flies.

This is a small town, Midnorth we call it. Tho originally we used to spell it with a hyphen — M,I,D, hyphen N,O,R,T,H; both the 'M' and the 'N' with capital letters. I suppose the founders named it that because they fancied themselves in the middle of the North. But gradually the thought-of sense to us of the name has changed. 'Midnorth' has come to mean, to us, not really in the North. For example, tho we're a small town, we've been incorporated as a city; and our population has passed the 20,000 mark. Still we still have something of a smalltown attitude and some room for pity. Even tho some of our newcomers (some of our old-timers too) advocate that we are now a growing city — practically big — and ought to forget about pity. Come to think of it, some of our old-timers never had any pity anytime. This is all right just to express an opinion; but what if you're the Town Clerk — or 'City Clerk' — like I am? He's been on the toot for ten days now and I still haven't fired him. Let the mayor fire him if he thinks Midnorth is a big city. In fact, every time he's phoned up for an advance I've given it to him — out of my own pocket too. I suppose that'll finally mean I'll have to wangle a bigger salary for him — when and if he comes back — so he can pay me back. And then some of them will call that corruption; in spite of the fact he hasn't gotten a raise for six of those seven years.

How do I know about those seven years? I certainly haven't looked it up in the records. This is a typical Canadian town and nobody gives a damn about records — doubtful that they still exist. What he did was stand on the corner of First Street and First Avenue (formerly Pioneer and Rob Roy Streets); stop people and tell them he was on a toot. He was sorry as all hell, felt really guilty about it, but he just had this toot coming. Then he'd say "I worked on the garbage for seven years . . ."

The way he said it had a sound like he was almost proud of it. So he should be, I say. Imagine sticking to a job like dumping garbage for seven years! I wouldn't stick to it for seven days, with two days off for a five-day week. Hundreds of Indians hanging around here with not much to do. Think one of them would do it? They won't and I don't blame them. But then, I have a family and friends in this country: so have the Indians — he's from Ireland.

So he kept telling people "I worked on the garbage for seven years." And sooner or later one of them would give him something, money or tobacco. He never asked for it. They just gave it to him. Then some of those who never gave it to him saw him getting something. So they said he was panhandling. These were for the most part the kind of people who wouldn't talk to him anyhow; and he wouldn't talk to them either. I don't blame him. I wouldn't talk to them myself if it wasn't my job to talk to everybody.

As I said, there's about 20,000 people in this town. That makes about 5,000 families. More or less. Now the funniest thing about all this is that a majority of people don't even know he isn't picking up their garbage any more. Most people don't know who's picking up their garbage . . .

The Garbageman is Drunk

Imagine having the same man picking up your garbage for seven years and not knowing who it was! Yet these same people, however, would think it funny — or at least very democratic of them — to know the man who's been picking up their garbage. As a matter of fact I think the reason the mayor has said nothing about it, is not telling me to fire the man, is *he doesn't know the man,* let alone know he's been picking up the garbage — or that he's been on a toot for ten days. Meantime the problem is mine — and that of the rest of the Public Works Department. Every day I've got to ask one of the men to take a spell on the garbage truck. Every day I've got to listen to that man's grumbling. They think it's an awful imposition, being asked to pick up the garbage for one day; when the garbageman's been doing it for seven years. I suppose when I rotate around the list of men I'm entitled to ask, I'll have to fire the guy. It would be useless to ask Manpower to send me a garbageman's helper for two or three days — useless to him that is. It'd cost whoever it was more money than he'd make. This is what some of those bureaucrats at Manpower never seem to get through their heads.

And a silly idea keeps going through my head. Except I don't think it's silly. Why don't *I* put on some overalls and go to help on the garbage truck? It wouldn't hurt me. I've tried to keep in shape but I'm lazy at it. It takes a good job of real work to make me bend my back. Work is what I'm used to, I'm not good at play.

Then you may ask (I hope you wouldn't ask this but I'm afraid you might . . .)

"Why should you take on such a dirty job?" Even for a day or two? Even though the knowledge I was doing it (it wouldn't cause such a big pile-up in my work; Midnorth is not that big a city) Even though the knowledge would cause the fellow to straighten up all the sooner?

People are always telling me I've got a peculiar way of

The Garbageman is Drunk

thinking; but I think these people who tell me that are kind of peculiar themselves — peculiar in a conventional way, peculiar like the whole country is peculiar. Collecting garbage is not a dirty job. On the contrary it's a clean job. Keeping the town clean is the cleanest work you can get.

Wouldn't want to do it all my life, though
Wouldn't want to do any one thing
so long it's as if you become that thing.
I'm damn sick of being Town Clerk,
or City Clerk,
or any title
you'd call me by and make me.
Feel like I was canned and labeled,
forgotten and set on a shelf forever . . .
And inside the can I'm
deteriorating, becoming something that's neither myself or the product advertised.

When the Ship of Villainy Went Down

When the ship of villainy went down
The last officer, clinging to a masthead
Screamed "There is no God!"
I figured it . . . Honest men were fools!
I could live by villainy all my life!
And now this horrible situation proves it!
There is no God! There is no God!

Upon which (he dreamt or maybe saw)
The sky unzipped like a tentflap
And a dusky chap — perhaps a Newfoundlander
Looked thru to say :
                              "B'ye
How be's it ye're complaining?
Haven't ye lived by villainy
All yer life?! "

To the Canadian Ruling Class

Me and Joe, over a beer
Have guessed your guilty secret . . .

You are not Canadians
(how could you be
when nine-tenths of the country
is no way occupied by you)
You're just claim-stakers
    — in fact claim-jumpers —
Sometime administrators
But mostly just purveyors of territory.

When an Eskimo is punished by his people
For a crime   —
                    You come along
And punish the punishers
(lately winning a liberal reputation
for not being so severe
on the dealers of justice)

Thus putting a color on the map
Of that territory as yours
So you can sell it later
At a profit which
                   Is
                   Actually
A hundred percent
Since you never owned it.

           That's
           Your
           Secret

           And . . .
           There!
           It's out!

In the Sky

The hawk swoops down upon three crows
But the crows have seen him;
Suddenly they become nimble
Their erraticness an advantage.

To the hawk's life, they'll give no tribute of death
                    They attack and
In half a minute it's over.
Knowing the slightest tremor of the wind
The hawk can climb faster.

Soon the crows have forgotten
Will tell no stories, sing no songs of triumph.
Neither does the hawk know humiliation;
Skimming, finding the updraughts
He distances further and further
Smaller and smaller in the heights.

Tho he must find a victim or die
Urgency's no use to him.
He's not equipped to think of it.

Wars Have Been Fought Over Less

Wars have been fought over less than two men Indian and
     White
Sitting in a restaurant in a town alleged
To be called 'The Meeting Place' in some old language;
The Indian with his head sunk sideways in his shoulder
The White Man saying, "What's the matter?"

"Nothing's the matter . . ."
"Then why are you so sad?"
"I'm not sad, just quiet . . ."
"What's the matter? Did I say something wrong?"
"Not until just now . . ."
"Nothing's the matter —
                 I'm reminiscing . . .
                      (You'll note

That he spoke in a strong tribal accent,
And 'reminiscing', tho a rare word in English
Probably corresponded roughly
To a common word in his language . . .
Also you'll note he didn't say
"*Just* reminiscing" . . .

The White Man, as White Men always will,
Persisted; as White Men always will persist
Til they give up and turn to alcohol
Or something   —   Til the Indian got mad
Tapped his skull and said, "Look
I've got something here
That's all my own . . ."
After which there was not understanding
But at least understanding that there was no understanding . . .

And as the two were face to face,
Both poor   —   no money to steal
Or property to seize as war reparations;
It ended there

England

England's a cretin's grunt dressed up in a crumbling gothic
Whose spires are spikes aimed at the curdling heaven,
Curdling, going rotten, and so close you can guess
Why its inhabitants once thought aiming their barbs that way
Required just a "Tally-Ho" and no mental effort.

England's a Lewis Carrol chessboard with all
      Shakespeare's characters
Overwhelmed in a sudden protracted deluge of applause,
      fossilized in their most sententious poses
With, crawling among the statuary, the English workers
Whining of how they're the slaves of Capital;
Contemptuous of anyone who's not a slave of Capital.

England's not the source of all our woes, just the source of
      the most annoying ones;
Where the aspiring-to-be-bright aspire to be gentlemen
Only to discover this is the contemporary age —
      there are no gentlemen.
Trained to administer colonies, they discover with surprise
There're so few colonies left the competition
Is so fierce it's like a river full of crocodiles —
      no other edible beast in sight :
So they come to Canada and other naïve places
To administer the colonies of the American Empire.

England is. England is. England is. If you want to put it
      into words
You've got to be drunk as Churchill was most of the time;
A place where every good resolve erodes in a gruel of
      bad oratory,
A rotten Stilton cheese mecca to expatriate Englishmen
      down to the sixth and tenth generation
Who dare not proclaim their loyalty with their own flag
But invent the Red Ensign and similar bastard rags
Which on various chickenpox scars of Earth denote
      the inhabitants
Continuously held-back coughs of submission to a
      dead-and-gone slavery.

7/7/71

Ode to the Timothy Eaton Memorial Church

You get up on that cross / This time Brother . . .
A carpenter, you say, gave up His life for you
And another carpenter knocked together
Two stout sticks . . .
          How charming were the Proletarians of Old Times!
I'm afraid us modern crew can't manage
That kind of mental weather;
If what you cross your hearts with crossed fingers
To say is true

          To save your souls?
How quaint! Take me for instance
     — I'd like to stand in for the Devil on his day off :
How I'd stoke!
               Or
                    To take a better image
With what gusto I'd stand on the podium / And wield my baton
To direct the instruments manned by the fiends of Hell —
Moans! Screams! Choked prayers and sincere curses!
     What cacophony! ! !

Don't twitch!
          Here's your crown of thorns Sir!
Bravely bear the royal pricks! You know
You were right —

That vision of a decent Man
A Good God even
Bearing all sorts of pains for the sake of sinners,
Or to put it more bluntly   —   the rich;
Does give a certain satisfaction
I'd say a certain peace of the spirit
As long as a few amendments are made
Like, You, the guilty
Suffering instead of the innocent . . .
Much as you lust for a pure paschal lamb
Paschal snakes are much more satisfactory
To me . . .
That's right!
Don't be shy!
Lick off that bloody sweat! ! !
In such circumstances the tongue's better than kleenex,
Like candy on an exasperating day :
And while you're tasting that Savour   —   My small mercy
— ponder on what your lying legend of a
Voluntarily
Suffering Christ really means

The Mine is also of Nature

The mine is also of nature. Take coal for instance:
Once it was a swampy forest (still smells like a
      swampy forest)
Was one forest after another, growing and falling,
      growing and falling;
Also falling piecemeal, shreds dropping off each time it
      was growing.

Why speak of the old you say? The old was once new
. . . New plants crawling from the shoreline, as worms
      would follow
For in those days plants crawled like worms;
Finding new places like the old, but stiller
Where all of nature that was busting within them.
As a heart hammers lifetime long at the ribs, a fist to
      a door;
All nature busting within could expand itself, experiment,
      grow and wander as a man
      grows and wanders in his dreams
Til where odd bits of green
Had floated or sunk, tasted top, tasted bottom;
A forest grew, high in the soughing wind, higher into
      the light.

The mine's a thing of nature. Sometimes those sparky
      demons — cones of light
Jumping in front of wherever their foreheads turn
— eyes glittering, savage stars on black faces
                 (no white men down here)
First one of those eyes — a corner — then the pair
'Il see the perfect imprint of a leaf, a precise wing
An insect dropped when itself dropped; or
Sometimes a blundering little beast
Maybe forefather or foremother
Of the body in which those eyes are fixed — near the
      top.

Why speak of the old you say? The old grows old in
        order to become new.
In a man's, a woman's, a child's mind, a thought
Twists itself into paradox
Strangles itself, rots
Until a new thought, richer — at least it ought to be —
        than the old;
Comes and shouts directions,
Heart gives chest a specially hard knock, the pecker
        swells, the eyes gleam.

Why speak of the old you say? A piece of coal
In its own way — its complexity as precious as diamond,
With enough pressure could become diamond
— nothing harder than diamond — at the very most of
        the least
There's bound to be some use found for coal.
Already thousands of things have been made of it
So why not keep the men digging? They do it, they
        enjoy it
As sailors love storms, as generals love battles,
As even soldiers itch for a just battle.
Against the pit of danger set the pit of boredom
Some love boredom, it's true — but not mountain
        climbers, not miners.

The mine is also of nature
And miners no less than farmers or Indians
People of the Earth, profound (profound means deep)
As a farmer shaves the younger surfaces, shaves them
        and digs in them,
The collier digs down to the ancient, surface after surface
Where there are trees, seeds. The Earth's hair has fallen
In a way continued to live, prepared and waited to live,
        retained forces like those of life
Until gathered, dragged out back to life (and if all this
        be true
Why not the lumberman? why not the barber?

Sometimes those salamanders, magical beasts full of fire,
        living as in fire, the people of the pit
'll come across a whole tree, fallen and pointed
As if ready to be picked up, used for a pencil
To write on the sky
"We   —   of this as well   —   are now inhabitants, a
        proportion, a catalyst . . ."
Sometimes they come on stumps still standing
Or roots still probing, even below the measures of the coal
Like the miner, who if he isn't the root
Is the sap, the life, the thinking reason for the root.

Where trees ran up, holed and porous for the sap
The mine, a mightier tree in reverse, runs down :
The ascending stem the descending shaft;
Roots spread over the flats and rolls of the surface;
Women, children, old men, boys sometimes frantic
Look about them, listen, converse, think and commit
        monkeyshines :
All too aware that they are roots.

29-31/1/72

54

Come Live with Me and Be my Love

Come live with me and be my love
Even if we've proven all the pleasures.
I'm standing on this wire and one good shove
Might toss me off. I need you. Be my love.

You complement me. What I see you see,
Often quicker. With you to watch my back, my front,
    my sides
I'll be tied firmer in the net of society.
Romantic — reasonably eternal — together we'll glide.

"A man without a woman is only half a man;"
The sages, quote by quote say things like this :
What if it's actually two-thirds or three-quarters?
You'll take what's left, mix and stir with womanly bliss.

After all it's true that you'll have children
And equally true that I have bigger muscles;
Right now you may be the cynic, but later
I'll be the one to warn you in the tussles.

Come live with me and be my love — it's inevitable.
If society no longer demands it, habit does.
You've got a light head and my shoulder's able
For use as a pillow while you complacently doze.

26/6/71

The Sleeping Giant

The Giant sleeps. Indians had no legends
Of him in old days. No wonder — he's a White Man
(small head : not much'um brains)
Though no good' Indian'd be so impolite
Even to think of such an under-rating;
Call us masters of evil, but
Masters . . . That's a compliment
(listen to Poundmaker on this;
he not only analyzes it . . . He advocates it)
If that's their way, the way which won, it must be the way.
His followers found it too damn stupid
Not just unnatual — uninteresting;
Did this thing, that thing

> but
> by and large

By and large
       BY AND LARGE
> nearby and very large

Remained in suspense but not sleeping;
Dreadfully not sleeping.

Across the Harbor from Thunder Bay
There's an island shaped like a mummified pharoah
From which the Egyptians used to remove brains
Not seeing any use for them (like the modern yanquified man)
And altho there's no sign of a pillow
Still it's called THE SLEEPING GIANT.

One night long ago, in his cups
An Indian was asked for its legend
Which, seeing he was a guest and drinking free
He provided gratefully.
Since then it's been a White legend
Which Indians took up in turn, elaborated
Always with the theme of *strange greedy men.*

On a clear day when the wind blows right
So that badge of oppression and conflict, smog blows away,
At sunset you see the Giant has many colors;
One of them White, one an eye-glutting Red
But overall and generally Blue
To signify we're all niggers here
Who work when permited, starve when told there's
        nothing else to do.

We've never had a good Prime Minister;
Get alcoholics, eunuchs, faggots
Whom Imperialists can destroy in a moment —
        if they act up,
Or stupid-but-honest men like Diefenbaker.
There's no Oom Paul Kreuger in our history;
Never a master, masters have been elsewhere
Tho we've had lots of Smuts'

Sleeping Giant
                :
                What kind of pill did you take
That you sleep and we have nightmares?
Mister Poundmaker, you were wrong :
Not all infected with disease
Are the disease   —   tho some are
Treating us little better than they treat you.
We're victims, and the masters are too
Which is no reason for not smashing them.
Wouldn't you wreck a dangerous robot?

On the waterfront at Thunder Bay
Late in November men, some Indian, mostly White
Are found frozen stiff as the Sleeping Giant,
        trucked away like garbage.
Later in winter there's no such problem.
Those who were going to freeze have frozen.

31/5/72

The Triumph of Art

On Saint Clair Avenue, in a three-room apartment
Antoinette (two sisters, three brothers)
has just the same found a corner where the impacts
of twisting bodies   —   tho you could still describe them
as innumerable   —   are nevertheless fewer than elsewhere.

It's not enough for her to say, "Life's more than this!"
After each collision   —   several moments after   —
That's just self-told cant. It isn't.
But when the spell leaves her circumstance
And goes into the pencil she's holding, the paper
        she's pressing down
Life *is* more . . .

Sometimes she gets up, eyes distant as her body's erect
Possibly she finds the toilet empty, possibly
she can lock herself in, possibly for some time;
where in a romance she half-way knows is romance,
        and half-way
doesn't care :
                She reads her poems aloud

23-27/6/71

My Love's Been Bitten

My love's been bitten by a Canada Goose.
Shall I get after him with my boots?
An animal doesn't understand the principle of revenge.
I can hurt him in body but not in mind
So what's the use?

I didn't (for this I feel guilty)
Kiss or soothe the spot;
It was (I'll try to explain)
The suddeness of her startlement;
The curve of her body when she tried to jump away
And after — the new curves when she was hurt.

In short. I am a bastard.
Never did I love her more than then
(all this happened many years ago;
and I still feel grateful to the goose . . .

The Schooner Blue Goose

It was the schooner Blue Goose, sailing in a race;
The captain had sold his country's honour (in Canada
    small disgrace)
The Yankees who had bought him say   —   and many say
    they're right
You can always buy the champion if you can't win
    the fight . . .

But when the Yankee started to pass, the Goose's onearmed
    mate
Let out a most poetic oath that froze the captain tight
(for no one is supposed to curse, on a schooner under sail
unless he is the captain   —   or doing the captain's will)

That I'm told   —   it may be a joke : but anyway everyone
    froze
In poses like a picture, each pointing with his nose
You can guess which way . . . the mate threw a right hook
    that crushed the Yankee plan
For no one can hit harder than a onearmed sailing man :

It is the rule of a onearmed man, if he's got blood to brew
He'll do more work with that one arm than other men
    can with two :
The champions of the onearmed man are onearmed men
    of the sea
The champions of onearmed seamen are men of the interface

Where the faces of two seas meet   —   the sea of the ocean,
    the sea of the air
Where we all live, since we're upstanding ocean   —
    ocean candy
   —but it's the occupation of sailors (men of sail)
To live and move by virtue of the fact that those two
    joined surfaces are
Moving against each other, in contradiction;

They live by contradiction, as we all do, the thing is to
      realize
as sailors develop a special skill of the body
and onearmed men develop a special skill of the body
. . . the swing and way of it; when to go easy and
      when to be sudden . . .

The schooner Blue Goose won that race   —   won it
      by several tacks;
Won that race with the captain lying unconscious
      on deck . . .
After'ds the captain went to the mate, said;
      "Though I lost my bet
I'll forget the whole thing if you will also forget!"

What could the first mate say? The law is rigid as hell
When you are sailing (clause after clause) you obey
      the captain's will . . .
They have such rules, over most the earth,
      even when there's no reason : —
Drive it to you twice as hard when there are
      facts to seize on.

The captain remained famous : —— His opinions quoted often;
The sea is not what it used to be . . . Men have started
      to soften
Since the unions ended the rule   —   each seaman on his own
With no consideration but the fact of master and man.

But I'll tell you another fact : that captain was laid
      full-length
By a onearmed first mate who made his weakness strength;
Who was no individual tough . . . but a Red   —
      and for the union
(you've got to reckon with men like him   —   if you say
      this country's done)

The Sea

Limitless sea? A lie! The sea's limited
To a variousness — nothing it's ever been can be repeated.
The light striking the water now, here, an hour before sunset
Makes it the color of a pale Chinese ink
But such a precise   shade of Chinese ink has never existed
Nor will any part of the sea be that precise shade again.

Infinity and finitude play loop-the-loop.
The sea, in every moment of all its ages
Has been different from anything it's been
And different from anything it'll ever be.
Repetition is impossible   —   no painting, no matter how
        truly
It catches the rage, the play, the calm of the sea
Is anything like the sea can possibly be
Yet there's no limit to its possibility
Even tho there're things the sea can never be.

No wave can ever duplicate another. The wavelets,
The weaving cross-hatches on the great waves
Can never cover one wave as they cover another;
The droplet of spray never flies from the same place
(how could you fix it as the same place?)
It rises. It roars. Like monstrous teeth
Its sudden upflingings threaten the atmosphere which
        torments it :
And its colors change, its loops and traps change.
        It'll never be the same.

25-26/6/71

The Rain—Trip

Take a rain-trip. Neither swallow it or smoke it,
But stand out in the rain, in shorts a loin-cloth or naked
With every aperture of your body open
And your thoughts a bubble from horizon to horizon.

Think a while and the clouds will be giant spiders
With every raindrop, thru all the time of its course
A leg . . . These are million-legged spiders
With every contradictory current of the air
Bending each one of the millions of legs
In hazardous curves   —   so they dance.

Get the cool of it . . . The chance taste
Of drops the open-bellied wind throws at you :
Eyes can taste then: the exits for sperm and urine
Can taste, and if the orifice for words
Opens for some statement which never issues
What comes in is a rain of tastes . . . Each itself part
          of the statement.

And every gable, every cave can be forgotten. What there is
Is a division of the rain, each house-ridge an edge
From which the water slides two ways, thin enough maybe
To let the molecules be counted; a house is
A place under a shifting fabric of rain, veiled at the sides by
Droplets spilling as a new state of the rain-being
After many other states have been . . .

And the trees   —   forget them. See them as a staggering
Of the legs . . . Drops change and fall in a different order
Not even themselves, other things of their own kind.
See the spaces where the trees might be
If you saw it differently
As saris of rain in a changed condition;
Ghosts of the rain which will continue to rain
When the rain is gone   —   its memory

On Not Being Banned by the Nazis . . .

At one fairly recent date in my distinguished career in that eminent institution, The School of Hard Knocks, I was shocked dizzy by learning that the great German poet Rainer Maria Rilke — had never been banned by the Nazis. In fact they had promoted his works . . . despite the fact that Rilke counted the defeat of the German Revolution of 1919 as one of the great disappointments of his life. He'd left Germany, immolated himself — as if he was some sort of vampire — in a tower in Switzerland: where he devoted himself to poetry and let the rest of the world go by. This is proof that even Fascists can forgive: provided whatever you've done againt them is silly, inconsequential and didn't particularly harm them.

Rilke didn't live long enough for the Nazis to come to power, or even to show themselves as a serious threat. He thus had no chance or occasion to condemn them. Still this doesn't explain why the Nazis not only easily forgave his early political aberrations, but promoted him, idealized him as an expression of the 'immutable German soul' and so on —

And this Idolization, in practically the same terms, continues in West Germany today. The fact is that Rilke framed his poetic vision on such a high plane of abstraction, in such 'universal human terms', that he gave offense to nobody. The Nazis could easily represent his message as supporting their beastly philosophy.   So I think I'll write down a few simple rules which in fact I have been using for years. Not to assure that my poems would be banned by Fascists if they ever came to power in Canada . . . I used for years to write every single one of my poems with some rule of the academic critics in mind — to show that the best poems could be written by violating those rules. I cannot list all the rules I used to infuriate the University Critics. But they turn out to be just the rules which would get my poems banned by fascists, so assuring, if not my reputation, at least my good name.

So I'll state a few of the most important ones;

(a) Write your poems so as to give pleasure to your friends AND pain to your enemies . . .

(b) At every stage of your poetic career write some poems about exploitation and oppression, showing sympathy for the oppressed and exploited. Do this no matter what other trip you are on. Avoid, however, doing like Raymond Souster — letting your sympathy for the oppressed degenerate into a mere poetic device, not looking towards the end of oppression. In other words show not only sympathy for the exploited and oppressed but hatred for the exploiters and oppressors . . .

show the power of the exploited and oppressed to confound their enemies.

To take an instance of the same thing as Souster does — 'though probably much better than Souster ever did in that line . . . There's the famous quatrain by the younger and better Irving Layton . .

"A friend tells me I should not write
About the workers and their plight
For poetry like dress admits of fashion
And this is not the year for passion.

For years I could not tell Irving or anyone else why I didn't like those undoubtedly memorable lines.

Only recently did I realize that 'fight' also rhymes with 'write'.

(b2) If you are not in sympathy with the oppressed and exploited, at least do them one simple human favour will you?

DROP DEAD.

(c) Write about nature, be sensitive about nature, by all means. But avoid writing exclusively nature poetry. Do NOT. Repeat NOT defame mechanical things, science and technique as such. The present smothering effect on nature of the spread of mechanical civilization, is not due to science and technique. It is due to private ownership of the factories, the planning of production not for the needs and wants of mankind, but for making profits. In a properly organized society all these mechanical things would be in the background, facilitating a pleasant life, instead of choking it. Even as things stand at this writing there are 18,000 horses in the lower mainland of British Columbia — exactly the same number as in 1918. The airplane, the sportscar, the motorcycle and the spaceship have opened up dimensions of poetry which never existed before. As for the hideous noise they make . . . Properly speaking, it is not the machinery itself which is making that noise, it is the Capitalist System.

(d) Include in every possible poem one line or passage designed to give acute physical pain, or its equivalent, to any reactionary who might read it. Do this openly if you want. In fact be sure to sometimes do it openly, as some reactionaries are stupid. But a way that's even more fun is to include in it some line, using every device to make the passage beautiful and quotable — so he memorizes it and goes round for days repeating it to himself — and then — BANG . . . the implication kicks him in the balls of his soul — he suffers complete destruction of the personality and goes home to put a bullet through his imitation brains

. . .

Another method of doing the same thing is to do the opposite. That is to quote the most obvious and bourgeois-destructive truth in the baldest, most brackish form: so he, reading it, says, "Ahah . . . this Revolutionary Poet writes bad lines! " So he'll go around quoting it to show what a bad poet you are (there is a real art to this. No line, however bad, can be remembered unless there's actually something good to it. So you have to write it so that it's good, but in a way he doesn't notice) . . .

Anyway by this trick you get him repeating it so often it becomes a part of his thoughts.

He starts thinking in the very terms he'd been deriding . . . and BANG! Same result. Perhaps either sort of such a line as I've described above will actually reform him; which is scientifically better than killing him.

It's always useful to have some Revolutionaries around who were once Reactionaries and have at least some remote memory of how a reactionary thinks. The surest way of knowing your enemy is to make one of those enemies a friend.

(e) In writing love poetry write as if the loved one had some existence outside of the poet's ego. For instance, don't do as described in:

ON THE LOVE POETRY OF CERTAIN MONTREAL

ANGLO POETS   (apologies to Roy Campbell)

> They praise the belly and they praise the breast
> They publicize the pubic curl --
> They praise the action, praise subsequent rest
> But where's the bloody girl?
>
> Milton Acorn & Maxine Gadd

Do do rather like . . . Well, I'm on the horns of that famous fighting bull EL DILEMMA. The bourgeois seldom does things by halves. In addition to counting their lovers as merely part of their own ego-trip, they also tend to put all of the great globe itself, which doesn't suit the particular thing they're occupied with at present, outside the barricades of their ego. Once the bourgeois fashion was to be 'impersonal'. So practically everything written down poet-fashion in those days was impersonal, in fact, unreadable. (They got their audience by becoming English Professors and prescribing their own books, and those of their cronies, for the courses they taught, exploiting students in the most direct way.)

Now the fashion has changed. The fashion is to be personal. So bloody personal there's only one person in the poem: the poet. And even that well-concealed behind a brush-fence of stances and poses. This thing's spread pretty far, and even poets who consider themselves revolutionary, even in the political sense like me, still are tainted by this fashion. What I'm trying to tell you is that the situation is so bloody awful there's hardly anyone I can give as an example but myself.

So *do* do like:

YOU GROWING

You growing and your thought threading
The delicate strength of your focus
Out of a clamour of voices
Demanding faces and noises
Apart from me but vivid
As when I kissed you and chuckled.

Wherever you are be fearless
And wherever I am I hope to know
You're moving vivid beyond me
So I grow by the strength
Of you fighting for your self, many selves
Your life, many lives. your people '

Write something like that and you'll get on a thousand academic blacklists. To be consulted and acted upon by the Nazis when and if (it's a big 'if') they come to power. It directly challenges every secret precept of the academics. The reference to 'growing' is especially poisonous to them — as all the Yeatsy-Wait-Sees and Ezra Pounders look on life as a process of decay. By fierce and irrefutable implication it condemns the systematic murder of student personalities, abject truckling before 'superiors', vicious dogmatism towards 'inferiors', rapacious slavering pursuit of money, lying calculated and feigned blindness when faced with any serious question —

In short, everything they hold dear.

(f) Try my rule . . . Write almost every poem so as to prove the vicious absurdity of university criticism. Do NOT, however, make this an excuse for mad poetry — poetry that is technically bad. Remember that poetry, like carpentry, is a craft. Learn every technical thing about it you can.

This is getting to be a furiously personal thing with me.

A fury inspired by exasperation and boredom. Time after time, when a young poet hands me one of his treasured products for comment, I have to take out a pen and start marking and underlining one elementary technical error after another. And what am I? A grammar school teacher? The errors I point out could have been learned by the young poet in half a day had he bothered to buy one book on the elementary rules of poetry.

It's true that ultimately all rules in poetry are made to be broken, but before you can break them successfully, you must learn that they exist, and *why* they exist. As old Satchmo once said about the anti-music of Dizzy Gillespie, ''You have to learn to play awfully good before you can play that bad! ''

I don't advise reading 'advanced books of poetry', I don't know what it is about the 'advanced books of poetry', unless it's that they're written by bourgeois-minded poets who are less concerned with passing on information than they are with hiding professional secrets.

This must be about the hundredth time I wrote an essay damning the 'academics' all to hell. Yet never before have I even considered publishing one of these screeds. Always there was a question in my mind which stopped me, ''What do I mean by 'academic'?''

After all the fascist poet, Ezra Pound, who continues to pass off his preposterous, common and dull *Cantos* as very profound, also condemned academics. The fast-rising Canadian patriotic poet, Robin · Mathews, is a professor. Pound was not.

Obviously, when I was saying 'academics' I meant something else.

I now realize that what I meant was 'Imperialist Academics' —

such as Northrop Frye, who in the past did more than any other one man to abolish everything native and non-European in our literature.

With the passage of Canada from a colony of England to a colony of Lower America (the U.S.A.) things have reached such a state that even imitation of imperialist models is frowned upon. American poets are sometimes permitted to think, sometimes *say* something of significance. Canadian poets must not, on the pain of immediate critical displeasure, even suggest they have a brain. B.P. Nichol actually hides his good poems (for posterity one must presume) and publishes masses of garbage about some figure of his private mythos called Captain Canada. Nichol's 'Captain Canada' makes no sense, thus passing on the very esoteric message that Canada makes no sense. For this he has been awarded the 'Governor General's Prize',

On an even higher plane of dullness, as fertile as the mountains of the moon — not those in Africa but on the Moon itself — stands George Bowering, personal puppet of Warren Tollman (whose name I might be mispelling but I don't care) a 'landed immigrant' professor in B.C. who after fourteen years' residence has never bothered to make himself a Canadian. Bowering's poems have to be read to be believed . . . so incredibly bad, so filled with faulty observation, so marked by such an absolute lack of any sense of proportion or humour;

that they too have gotten the 'Governor General'. Bowering and Nichol are good colonial boys — without a thought in their heads which they will reveal. At least publicly they leave all the thinking to their Imperialist bosses.

People like these, and there are many like them, are what I mean by 'academics' although Nichol in fact has no university connection.

Neither did Ezra Pound, or Rainer Maria Rilke.

The Big Saw

Many's the time when I was on the job
The sawman came to me :
"You're able   —   And you can work fast.
Why don't you handle the big saw?"

Upon which I'd hold up my hands
Thumbs and fingers spread out :
"Look. Count 'em. Ten isn't there?
That's how many there's going to be!"

The Universe and I

Signs in the skies. It isn't God has been at work.
It's artisans. Spacemen and their master helpers
Play parchesi with the constellations. On a clear night
Here thru a windy blanket we
See the new stars fly, north, south, east, west
     — and all angles between. Who has noticed this?
Satellites and their discarded fragments — space junk.
The eternal heavens have vanished in our time :
Again I ask you.
               Who has noticed this?

Alienation. A word which mixes and crosses
With stupidity. Cultivated stupidity. Cultivated by
        the master class.
Don't notice the Revolution is spreading. To make sure
        of this don't notice anything.
Last year there was something white and bright in the sky
Large-headed, short-tailed, visible in daylight
I saw it. My mother saw it. We wondered what it was.
When it moved around to the nightside
Somebody noticed. Named it Bennet's Comet.

But who am I to say this? More observant than most
Still our ancestors would've seen it immediately.
I'm a man of my age. Can't escape. Think sometimes for
        years
Before the obvious occurs to me

There is a Prufrock shallowly interred in me;
Most of what you see is myself
But the tip of a nose, a little finger, an earlobe
That's Prufrock. Why don't I learn to speak fluent French?
Not hesitate before going swimming?
Collect a library and research
Before lips flap and typewriter clacks?
Sometimes I wonder . . . is Prufrock a tumor in me
Or am I an itch on Prufrock?*

Still I collect the lives of great men
And identify myself with them.
In other lands ambition's no longer appropriate . . . Here it is.
(I think of Cincinnatus, appointed dictator of Rome
In a crisis, and when it ebbed
Was offered a sinecure with great honor.
He said, "My fields have been neglected . . . Need plowing."
How I'd like to be like him!
                              Go back to the trade.
            I represent something.
                                    Can't do that.
In these days it's an idle fantasy.

Wouldn't it be fine to see my cortex rise in the East
Like one of those newfound galaxies
With lightrays coming out like drills and corckscrews!?
The eye struck and penetrated — right to the brain!
One look — instant wisdom!
One look at my poem — instanter wisdom!
And all who see it able to duplicate . . . There's ambition
        for you! ! !

* Main character in THE LOVE SONG OF J. ALFRED
PRUFROCK — a hilariously funny bit about a middle-
class present-day Hamlet, written by T.S. Eliot, whose
admirers insisted on taking him seriously. Because of this
occurred one of the most astounding cases of possession in
poetic history. All Eliot's subsequent poems were written
by J. Alfred Prufrock.

She Defines Herself Early

Growing old, like drop by drop
Of clear fluid dripping from her mirror
She loses her beauty. At the very time
When in men's eyes she's gaining
That presence in herself, that eclaire
Which we define by many names, ashamed to say "beauty";
She examines her looking glass
As a general would examine a map
And mourns *"it isn't there! not there! there no more!"*

She defines herself early; as a young girl. Slavery. Sticks to that.
(the grip of the master (even when she's one of the masters)
(the mind-worm sucking thoughts (self conquering self)
Is a matter of stasis, static definitions
Are necessary, not to us
But to the machine playing its own games
Instead of our games . . . with us.
Mindless itself, lacking that world within
— the world without known first as the world within
It reflects its non-thought as our thoughts.

The beautiful woman sits alone. Here there's a
                          double misunderstanding.
Brought up to b'lieve in gods (and of course
every man and in fact woman
in her den of secrecy means 'goddess')
; here's a goddess. One doesn't approach Godhead
Up on the feet . . . Convention and the liquor laws
Forbid crawling — besides prayers are necessary
And precisely what's most forbidden
Both by atheism and religion
Is sincere prayer — after all the only kind.
As for the woman all she thinks is
                         "I'm getting old! ?"

So a grudge grows . . . And like most grudges
Revenge hits the guiltless instead of the guilty.
So one hears : "you only (sic) want to screw me!"
Maybe he only wants to worship
And how d'yu do that
With no hope of entering the shrine?
Too much of us is clay. We are too easily
        moulded by words;
Define ourselves by terms
Which in this alchemy become obscene
Tho many languages have no obscene words
. . . in fact no such word as 'obscene'.

27/1/72

The First and Last Centennial of the Royal Canadian Mounted Police

Inspector Horseman, Horses-In-Absence, Mister Equus Sir
When you engaged in a gay back-slapping match
     (red hands on red tunics)
With American gangsters; combined with them
To crush the Canadian Seamens Union
Did you imagine you'd silenced all voices in all time thereafter
So no gunbarrel of a poet's finger would ever aim at you?

Consider the horsefly, how he sits and bites, sucks, flies off
Becoming in imagination many other things
But remains in mind and body in many more ways a horse
So he walks clank-clank-clank, exactly as if ironshod;
And ever after, when he speaks, must modulate his tone
Lest a sudden unwilled neigh betray his horse-hormones

Inspector Horsesweat : did you have faith in an immutable God
Of evil sitting on a throne built from history-books with
     blank pages?
An iron bit of silence on all tongues for all ages?
So nobody would ever yell, "You're the one
Who combined with American gangsters to crush the Canadian
     Seamens Union."?

Inspector Horsehide, Horsemeat, Mister Dogfood Sir
: I'll admit knowing what you already know
That a combination of policemen and gangsters is neither rare
Or paradoxical. Your noble duty
Is to maintain the system which maintains gangsterdom;
That yours has been a centuries-long sham battle
Against the condition of man which you make possible.

I'll pronounce the name of the Canadian Seamens Union
Without pity : with glory on my voice;
For under the combined attack of you, Inspector Horsepurs;
American gangsters plus all other
Sanctified and religious powers,
With fifty-two ships and their crews (52)
It tied up most of the world's major ports.
No U-Boat Fleet ever cleared the seas
As did the Canadian Seamens Union.
Inspector Horsetail you'll be remembered
Only when the Canadian Seamens Union is mentioned.

She . . .

The frame's of ebony, it is a door
, a place to look where she pre-empts the spaces
because her hair, because she is
             as waves in those spaces . . .
Nothing about her is quiet, no more than the moon
on a night of meteors . . .

You look into the frame as into a mirror gone wrong,
thinking that she isn't you   —
                         there are
                              steps
                                    made
                                        in
                                          the frame
; and you look for the scuffed shadows of her feet
Where she may have stepped, may step, may never step :
You have your thoughts and hers are a reflection
as yours are a reflection;
                  hers could be yours
                         and yours could be hers;
but how do they swirl in her brain now
as if they were yours?

Thinking of the frame as a door, the door as a frame
                                                    and you
in the room as a frame, the frame as a room
; the identity of I and you
. . . her dress steps into the eye as blue while you're thinking
of clouds moving across her eyes, as you;
and there are mites of life

                        cells struggling through her eyes
                        like you
: thinking of this, and her, you are
words yourself   —   a sentence dropped halfway through
and thought of   —

A sentence that is me; a sentence I complete and think
        you said
; a sentence answering itself
                                while the tongue hangs as a cloud
And her mindseye moves as in a cloud, and you

Of souls the most near are the most mysterious . . .
Nothing so mysterious as her presence
in herself, and with you
as a term in her spaces . . .

7/7/71

Bob Atkinson's Poem about an Empty Cigar—Box

Brown is the color of somebody's truelove
And of the box out of which Bob Atkinson gave me
  his last cigar . . .
White is the color of another truelove
Or black or flushed with copper or faint gold;
Hearts are red and souls striped like tiger-bodies
While the birthmarked girl is lovely if she thinks so : —

Railway-passengering thru Fraser Gorge under a quarter
  moon,
The crinkle on the water, the dead breadwhite that shines
Has the horror of corpse teeth; one visualizes this very train
Black, broken like a miserable kid's toy
Indistinct, curved with gaps and snaggles in the vile water
And white spit scarcely spilt about it : —

Float down! Bob Atkinson's cigar-box! Through the
  Fraser Gorge!
Full of roses, forget-me-nots, thorns and tools of precision!
Perfume of roses to shine instead
Of the kind of shining there is not after moonset
And splashes from the raging water for dewdrops
  to miniaturize the red dawn . . .

Bob Atkinson works a fifty-hour week —
Paid good for it, they would say (But who could be paid
  for a 54-hour week
Well?) Puts in forty or more hours a month for the
  credit union
Unless a dollar or a nickle gets mislaid
When he works more :   — Despairs that his class
Will ever rule, or even that it should rule :
Says his brothers are happy with material wealth,
Looks happy himself, but knows he isn't . . .

There is the problem of love which is true
And in a certain sense never ends — gets truer forever . . .
But in a certain sense, certain things
Can be done too many times . . . The children are grown,
        the parents are still young :
First love can occur again and again
And divorce is easy now — just for the rich . . .
And why divorce? What has been the tragedy?
Must all be official? Officially bitter? Official meaning
        bitter?
The great actor moves through commanding the picture
As death in a medieval painting commands the tattering
        corpse of the live man
As Errol Flynn walks in on the Blue General
And the general is flustered, a martinette, a good one,
        a bad one;
In short his movement is that of an eraser on an upside-
        down pencil
And scene by scene it waggles and rubs, the bit players
        are turned to fragments of rubber dust —

The star versus the bit player — the bit player
        versus the star —
Whichever role it is for me it still disgusts me
Unless I slt in a worker's kitchen,
Unless I come in from the snow to Bob Atkinson's door
Like Bobby Burns into a crofter's cabin —
The camera pans on me for a moment : —
Mary speaks to me, I get the message, I go shining : —
The plot goes on, there is a faint hum of peace,
        the projector whirring
While at the end of the fluttering beam as of a troubled
        sunrise in a hushed theatre,
The plot, the desperate plot goes on
To an end which is a   hopeful beginning . . .

Use Bob Atkinson's cigar box to pack poems
Fill it with marbles, fill it with pistol bullets,
       fill it with Habana cigars : —
Scrape Victoria off her pedestal, gently remove the
       pigeon shit
And set up Bob Atkinson's empty cigar box
For children to pitch shiney new pennies
At — Leave the pennies. What good are they for anything
       but pitching?
Always have shiney new ones on top —

The message was like something as if there was a hole
       in a screen door :
Scab products were getting through; someone is threatening
       somebody's living
    — screams in horror of any sacrifice
except the normal routine one to the Boss
by which all things are done, all run, all sanctified
by the cross-crisscross of dollars and bills
       of various denominations plus types;
substance for 50 per cent of the lectures, mostly in favor,
       day and night
    — someone is screaming "I have a right"
to sacrifice myself to any Boss on any terms —
And scab products are getting through; I will deliver the
       message
Even though because of my message, someone may even
       die . . .
For if I don't deliver the message someone else may die
And part of the hope, the hope beating like a heart
Wherever a heart beats   — it may die. It goes on.

In photographs of Red October and the months
And years after, the faces of the Bolsheviks, the way they
       stand with arms at angles, the way they turn to look
Acquire a terrible familiarity: — the people we know
       — not as we see them,
As we remember them, as we see them in our strongest
       dreams —

Lenin looks like a rough, except he has just washed his
     face
That's the way he always looks: — he has just
     washed his face —
No Revolution since has matched this . . .

All sorts of people ask me for poems
But if a worker asks me for a poem I never pale : —
This is class-consciousness, dirty class-consciousness
     if you wish;
Neither good nor bad but simply what I am
And if it saves this cracked up world   —   ?
                         The hammer
Which falls true   —   It's it which drives the nail;
And the tongue which is close to the mind,
     which is truthful :
Without it nothing happens right . . .
                      I've travelled
And know which men are truthful . . .
                    The workers :
And not only the workers.
               Such as
A Chinese scholar, cum laundryman, cum Revolutionary,
     cum poet sitting at the exit to the Yangtze Gorge :
Writing a poem about history, comparing himself to
     Genghis Khan
But with another thought, a thought more comparable
To who lives and who cries for life today;
Crying more broadly for life than Genghis
For there are more people in his thoughts   —   you see them
           in his calligraphy
(the calligraphy of Mao, where every character looks human,
whose poetry you could almost read, as *some* poem
     particular to you, even without knowing
     the language) . . .
Out of the rapids at the end of the Gorge swings and swims
     a brown cigar-box
With a brighteyed sparrow riding it for a boat,
Looking at you

Roseprick of which Rilke Died

Mourning for the living, mourning for you and I
Who didn't make my life material for disaster;
Subject to dolorous poems :
It was made for me — just that way.

A dreaming loon drifts on the waves
Up and down, their breaking no worse than snoring;
As I'd want to live — tell myself I should go from
                            love to love.
My brain's the rebel leader of my will . . . My body disobeys.

Roseprick of which Rilke died
I shan't die of you or any regret.
Emily? A few furtive screws was all she could get.
She actually calls them that.

Black thrushes in the wintriest weather
Fly in and out of nooks, protesting the cold;
Sometimes shrill but never far from song
Sometimes clear-noted as robins.

For a little while we lied. It was a stratagem
Against ourselves, hoping to let truth sneak 'round and in
Til our movements were no longer like dancers'
But of the last pieces in a drawn game.

24-1-72

Ho Chi Minh

. . . and still there is the final murderer;
men can't be women, or women men —
we can't be children again
if we were ever children;
nor can the dead become the living . . .

Imperialists, factionaries, gangsters
felt his heartbeats like beewingbeats
shaking their tailored hates, the rigidities of their minds . . .
Made plots when they only had to wait.
Such victories are guaranteed.

The child whimpering to silence
in ruins, the aborted baby;
these are, in their ways, greater losses :
for who can tell that sort of probability
and possibilities even greater?
but we knew this one
and his strength was ours . . .

To be like him? It
would be wrong to be like him;
only in certain things, chosen
and learned with equal bitterness, in later times.
Only he could be himself.

We shall never have this sword again :
We will always need it;
even when, instead of 'sword'
we may say 'flower'.

7/7/71

The Company Only Called Just Limited

The company only called just limited
                                    Listen
                                        It I encountered
It, it, it, it, it, it, it, it, IT, IT, IT
And the paint had an existential sheen grey
Which wiped out all the other words on the sign
On a warehouse on the waterfront at Victoria
(that color used for bumpers on a capitalist car
which actually couldn't outbump anything
at any speed faster than five miles an hour,
or the half-polishy color of tapwater running through
    — which maybe was the idea of the building's owner)
Some small enterprise had perished there
And that making-anything-seem-like -nothing color
        Was lying in wait for the next small victim

"Paper Tiger Enterprises" I thought
With a nod in the direction of Comrade Mao
Smile in the East! The whole Pacific Ocean with its
        horizon line
The shape of a guiltlessly confident smile
Altho the ends of the lips point down;
Altho in Victoria the perfectly understandable East
Is actually West . . . Such are the limitations of words.

Limited; limited; I'm so limited!
                            It makes me mad
That I could drown in a small arm of a big ocean;
A big arm of a small ocean : a lake so distantly related
        to an ocean
That only very limited maps record it
Or a puddle six feet six inches deep
As soon as I got tired of jumping . . .

Limited; limited; limited; limited!
                            What is *it*
            This thing that's so limited?
It^1; it^2; it^3; it^4; it^5; it^6; it^7; it^n —

There should be something done about a word
Which has such an unlimitedness of meanings
Like coupling it with 'limited' . . . Forming a corporation
      called "It Limited"
The whole business being to see that the copyright of
      neither word
Is infringed upon . . . Think of the lawsuits! The profits!
And no sillier than most of the ways
In which money is made . . .

'Yankee Acquisitions Limited" I might add
          The only limitation being
That as long as there are not *Commies/Reds* firing
      anti-aircraft missiles
At innocent Gringo warplanes that pass
Every stray piece of territory belongs to America :
Or "Definition Of America Limited"
Since they've limited that too
Even tho this place I happen to be writing
Is America according to any map . . .

Talk of your limitations! Recently
The Yankee oil-tanker-icebreaker "Manhattan"
Failed to make the Northwest Passage;
So promptly all the Yank-Pig-Newspapers (including those
      published in Canada)
Shortened said passage by several thousand miles
And *presto* the "Manhattan" had made it!
The "Sainte Roche" became second best.
That's limitation for you!

The Company only called just Limited —
Is at present very limited, limited to nothing;
Which frightens me, since nearly all the Universe
Consists of that . . . Absolutely nothing.
On the other hand let's let them have that :
All of nothing to belong to the Yanks . . .
Everything that's something for the rest of us.

1965-1971

87

The Second World War

Down Great George Street, up to the station;
The skirl of the pipes the very thrill of your nerves
With the pipemaster (only man who has the Gaelic)
Ahead with his great baton, his strut and toss proud
        as any man who's ever walked.
This is where we came in; this has happened before
Only the last time there was cheering.
So few came back they changed the name of the regiment
So there're no cheers now. Tho there are crowds
Standing silent, eyes wide as dolls eyes, but brighter
Trying to memorize every face

This is where we came in. It happened before.
        The last time was foolishness
Now's got to be done because of the last foolishness.
In the ranks, perfectly in step (with the pipes
        even I'm perfectly in step)
I'm thinking of THROUGH THE LOOKING GLASS :
The White King's armies marching while he sleeps;
We are his dream . . . At least it seems that way.
They're so clumsy the front line topples
The second line topples over it; and on it goes
        — line after line , eyes glazed straight forward
Shoulders back, spines held stiffly unnatural
Toppling over the line before

So few came back they abolished the regiment.
I was lucky — sickness and bad marksmanship.
Man by man we'd sworn to take our guns back,
        man by man we didn't.
One man — one war — that's all he's usually good for.
Now a strange short-haired subculture
Glares at us out of the TV set
Snarling the news, every phrase or disguised opinion
        as if it was a threat, which it is.
This is where we came in
It's happened before.
This last time was right
But ended in foolishness.
It has happened before.
                        It will happen again.
To end in foolishness?

What are the Odds ?

If we Canadians, following the programme advocated by many, but most clearly by the Canadian Liberation Movement, seized the foreign-owned industries in our territory —

and if the principal foreign owner, the American Empire, launched military operations against us; What are the odds? Would we win?

Simple arithmetic (say 200 million against 20 million — for the purpose of the argument counting Quebec as part, or more likely, an ally of Canada) give no reliable guide. History is replete with victories won by small nations over much larger ones: Greece vs. Persia; Macedonia vs. Persia; Greece vs. Italy; Albania vs. Germany. Politico-military factors, not just arithmetic, decide wars. Von Clauswitz, the acknowledged bourgeois authority on war, was as clear on this as is Mao Tse-Tung.

CANADIAN MILITARY PROWESS

First, one must consider that it is Canada, not so much the U.S., which is famed as the homeland of fierce and expert fighters. Twice this century, Canada has become involved in major wars. Even though the motives of Canadian soldiers were confused (more so in the First than the Second), they accomplished remarkable feats.

Perhaps most remarkable in the First World War was the Canadian performance in the air. Of the ten top 'British' aces, four were Canadian. Billy Bishop made such a mark that I doubt the 'second rate Canadian' propaganda has succeeded in erasing it from the minds of most readers. His official record is smaller than the Red Baron's but he may actually have shot down more planes. Most of his fights were over enemy territory and many of his victories not confirmed.

Von Richtofen himself fell victim to the Canadian ace Roy Brown. There is added drama here which our colonial culture-vultures have entirely missed. At the time of his own death 'Death's Adjutent' was pursuing Wop May, later to become the most fabulous of bush pilots.

He should be a Canadian legend as much as
    Bishop himself.
There should be a Canadian book about Richtofen
    called APPOINTMENT WITH BROWN.
Brown committed the fearful offense of putting
       PERIOD
       THE END
       FINIS

         To the career of a famous killer or hero of Im-
perialism. For that he has been consigned to limbo. How many
Von Richtofens did Eddie Rickenbaker shoot down? Still,
the Yankee flier is more famous than either Bishop or Brown.

It's not generally known that the Canadian victory at
Vimy Ridge was a turning point, not only in the history of
Canada, but of warfare. Here it was proved that a defense
line which couldn't be outflanked and was not surrounded,
could be taken by direct assault, although manned by
soldiers who had previously been considered the world's
most expert and steadiest.

Essentially, victory was won on the first day of all-out
infantry and artillery assault against overwhelming German
airpower. Canadian courage, Canadian dash played their role.

The main Canadian assault swept ahead as accurately as
a railroad timetable. No wonder, the troops knew the plan
to the last detail. Indeed, the whole army had been involved
in drawing up and perfecting the plan.

A few months later, our recent ancestors — many still
live to tell of it — concluded the horrible Battle of Passchen-
dale by actually winning some sort of victory after the
British army had been virtually destroyed. There is only
one word to say about that Canadian capture of Passchen-
daele Ridge– *impossible.* But history inalterably records . . .
it happened. History and veterans are reticent about just
how it was done. The world wants to forget the ultimate
waking nightmare of Paschendale . . . But the time has not
yet come when Canadians can afford to forget.

When the Canadian Corps reached the top of Vimy
Ridge, their conduct amazed German witnesses; those who
escaped and those who remained as prisoners. The ferocity

and vengefulness of Canadian soldiers is largely legend. What struck captured Germans was Canadian chivalry. The first question to many prisoners was: "Are you wounded?". The second; "Are you hungry?"

There was little cheering; the army simply stopped, milled around, and admired the fantastic view. This writer, who saw little action in the last war, nevertheless, was a witness and participant in another such incident, when Canadian soldiers aboard ship under torpedo attack, since they could do nothing, just stood on the decks and enjoyed the spectacle. Veterans of that war attribute the unquenchable Canadian morale to the morbid Canadian humour, a Chinese-like ability to see the funny side in everything. This is only one aspect of the Canadian capacity for forgetting oneself, even in the most desperate circumstances.

Like the players of Team Canada, in the midst of a close-played hockey game, with the prestige of the country at stake, forgetting the contest, rallying like a band of red guards.

Our People have amazing qualities.

Well — so have any People. But there's no harm in us concentrating on the particular positive qualities we do possess.

Like Newfoundlanders enjoying a secret joke, Canadian World War I veterans saw to it that war monuments in Canada were inscribed '1914-1919'. The nineteen-nineteen part refers not to the Treaty of Versailles, but to the fact that the last battles of the Canadian Expeditionary Force were fought not in France or Germany but in England: where the Canadians were held, kicking their heels, while efforts were made to recruit them for service against the Bolsheviks. Our men responded with a series of 'riots', so called, in which some were killed and some took wounds. A few survivors still actually draw pensions.

This is celebrated in an otherwise incomprehensible verse from *Mademoiselle from Armentieres:*

The little red train ran down the track
Parley-vous?

The little red train ran down the track
Parley-vous?
The little red train ran down the track
She hit the station a hell of a whack!
Inkey-dinky-parley-vous?
Parley-vous indeed! It means, "Are you on my wave-length?" "Do you understand?"!

All this we did despite the fact that Anglo-Canadian politicians seemed to be doing their very best to bring the war to Canada, to make it a civil war between the Québécois (then preposterouly called 'the French') and English Canadians. The Conscription Crisis was a colonial artifact . . . and as a matter of fact, resistance to conscription was as strong in British Columbia as in Quebec.

Had Canadians and Québécois started fighting each other in Canada (they did to some extent) they'd have likely fought each other in France too. Québécois might have played their part in the mutiny which overtook the French Army, probably making it a different kettle of fish. Québécois are not the worst, but probably the best fighters in the Canadian Army. Couldn't the Anglo politicos be content with that?

They weren't.

They were less concerned with winning the war than with fastening their yoke tighter on Quebec. History is full of might-have-beens.

In the Second World War, at least to official historians (who don't want Canadians to realize their capacities, being colonial compradors), the Canadian contribution was less spectacular. Apparently because a legend had grown up around the Canadians . . .

The rule was: "If a job looks impossible, send the Canadians. If they can't do it we know it's impossible." There was the case of the Scheldt Estuary, which the Germans had flooded. The Canucks had to wade from island to island, practically without cover, capturing them one by one, advancing along the dikes, eyeball to eyeball with the Nazi parachutists, fanatical youths, thoroughly indoctrinated with Nazi racial theory. And the Canadians won the battle.

How many know that the Battle Of The Atlantic was 50 per cent a Canadian Battle? Except for the sailors concerned, we didn't know that even while the fight was on! The record of the RCAF in fighter combat is even more obscure; perhaps because our men were delegated to flying Hurricanes, probably the worst fighter plane for its time of all time —

Canadian fighter pilots who made their mark mostly flew in the RAF, with Spitfires — another bad plane, as were all European planes of that day, but good enough to combat the preposterous Messerschmidt — which German fliers sarcastically called 'the flying brick'.

It had difficulty taking off, difficulty landing, and had an extremely short flying and fighting time. A good combat plane in all respects except one. It couldn't fly.

Against these Messerschmidts, flying the only slightly better Spitfire, Buzz Beurling, of Verdun, Quebec, scored 21 victories. Sometimes, during the Battle of Malta, Beurling's plane was the only 'British' craft in the air. The Germans feared him. The Imperial British hated him. Called him 'Screwball'; indeed the first word of his exploits to reach Canada were stories of a 'Captain Skruball'. He died mysteriously in a light-plane crash soon after the war.

Tales of other Canadian aces in the RAF are recounted only in family histories. One of these aces is said to have been shot down by the British!

The main exploits of the RCAF in World War Two were those of the pathfinder squadrons; bombers who flew ahead of the main bunch and marked the target. This terror bombing accomplished little more than to make the Germans mad — unite them behind the Nazis. Still it called for skilled and courageous flying and shouldn't be forgotten.

Canadian troops were used as cannon fodder in Normandy. Absolute insanity you say? Using shock troops for cannon fodder? Not so insane when looked at from the point of view of the Imperialists in command in the west. They had to think not only of winning the war but of winning the peace, and our men were notorious for their fanatical anti-Fascism.

Anti-Fascism? In the war between the wars, the war most unambiguously anti-fascist, the Defense of the Spanish Republic, Canadians contributed, on a per capita basis, the second largest contingent. Fighting against incredible odds, in a makeshift army using mostly makeshift weapons, we performed as well as anybody could expect.

In the only successful Loyalist offensive (cancelled out by a massive counterattack against Teruel), the Mac-Pap Battalion was among the first units to enter the city. In the retreats, the Mac-Paps succeeded in holding together, continuing to fight as a unit. That was rare.

Incidentally these Canadians, the first of our nation to oppose Fascism in battle, to this day get no pensions from the Canadian government. Neither are they entitled to treatment in veterans' hospitals. The Imperial dinosaur never forgets. It may do its damnedest to make you forget — but it forgets nothing, forgives no deed of justice.

In both World Wars, Canadian civilian effort was outstanding. Though in the Second it was hampered at first by a virtual strike of the bourgeoisie, who demanded and got greater profits. This is why there was still unemployment in Canada a year and more after the Second World War started.

I have laboured a point which seems minor perhaps too long. The fact is, any people on Earth, fighting a just cause, using correct ideology, (these days, Mao Tse-Tung Thought — somewhat contributed to by Norman Bethune — a Canadian), can accomplish military feats which astound the world. The example of Vietnam is always before us.

But the grip of U.S. Imperialism on Canada is ideological, is cultural, economic, every damned thing you want to think of.

The Imperialist legend is that all men are equal — *except Canadians.* Canadians are inferior!

I'm putting it this way because that's the way the liberal puts it. American Fascism doesn't take much hold on the Canadian mind. American liberalism does. Both sides of the border, small-'l' or big-'L', American and Canadian Liberalism are the same. Liberalism is a tool of Capitalists, Bureaucrats and Imperialists against the minds of subject and exploited peoples. Liberalism says first that Canadians are inferior. Then: "So we're inferior! So what! After all there are certain values which go along with inferiority!" You'd think they were talking of a primitive people.

History is leading to a Workers' Earth, and finally a classless society — true — but fought for through the Revolutions and Peoples Wars which are national. No lesson of history has been more profoundly impressed than this.

I'm talking of such a possible war, and must get back to the question of Canadian prowess in the bloody game. Bloody as the knife in Bethune's fingers . . .

CONTINUING REVOLUTION

The history of Canada has been a history of rebellions. Several are mentioned in Canadian history books, are played down and made to look like comic opera. Yet it might be argued that our history, since at least 1837, has been one of continuing Revolution, as yet incomplete, flaring here, flaring there, but always isolated or suppressed locally before it has a chance to become general.

The struggle in Ontario in 1837-39 was actually a very bloody one, considering the small population.

The Land Struggle in Prince Edward Island went on for over a hundred years. It was remarkable for its comparative lack of bloodshed, not because the Island farmers lacked militancy, but because they took care to arm themselves with muskets, a military weapon, rather than rely on the slow-loading rifles and shotguns of that day. Immediately after their victory, the Islanders were tricked and sold into Confederation (not the *founding* of our nation, but the ultimate sellout to Imperialism).

It has taken another century for Islanders to reconcile themselves to the fact that they are Canadians. Faced with a renewed Land Struggle, they are only recovering their legendary militancy today.

The latest rebellion was in this century. The fierce strikes which swept Canada in the 1920's and 30's reached their apogee on Cape Breton Island. Reading about the struggle, listening to reminiscences, legends still repeated all over the Atlantic provinces, one is forced to say: "That wasn't just a strike. It was Revolutionary War."

In one of the most treacherous turncoat deals in Canadian History (that's saying a lot), it was sold out by the Communist Party of Canada which turned the Steel and Mine Unions — avowedly Red Unions — over to John L. Lewis and other U.S.A. bureaucrats.

Not only Cape Breton was betrayed. All Canada was betrayed, since other strikes going on at the same time were also very savage. There was a widespread tendency for the petit-bourgeois to take the side of the workers, the very opposite to what was happening in the U.S. The mood of the Canadian proletariat was definitely pre-revolutionary and revolution often has not only a polarizing power but also a pulling power.

In these conflicts, both Patriots and 'loyalists' acquired a *military instinct* which has become part of Canadian culture and psychology. Such things are not abolished in two decades of negativating propaganda. Imperialism is simply incapable of changing the character of a people that fast. All Canadians have to do to recover it is realize it's there.

TWO ALLIES

The first attempt of the United States to become an imperialist power was stopped in its tracks by the supposedly inefficient Canadian yokels. In the War of 1812-14, the American armed forces alone outnumbered the whole Canadian nation. The British had little to do with our successful defense. They were fully occuped with Napoleon in Europe. It seems the French Imperialists and the would-be American ones had worked out a divvy-up-the-world scheme: the American attack on Canada and Napoleon's invasion of Russia came simultaneously.

Napoleon's invasion of Russia established one of the

primary rules of war in the present age: DON'T MARCH ON MOSCOW. It has gone unnoticed that the simultaneous American adventure established an equally valid rule: DON'T INVADE CANADA. The war of 1812-14 is not the only Yankee military incursion into Canada, only the most spectacular and determined one.

The politico-military factors which made for this astounding David vs. Goliath victory could operate for us today. Scratching out the British, Canada did have two important allies. One was the Indian Peoples, at that time making, under Tecumseh, their second attempt to recreate themselves as a nation. The other was the American Anti-Imperialist Movement.

Throughout America's history, her people as a whole have never been sympathetic, or at least really committed, to their bourgeois masters' Imperial ambitions. Practically all America's major wars have had to be represented as anti-imperialist. The Spanish-American War, the First and Second World Wars . . . When a rival Imperial Power doesn't exist, one has to be invented; Russia in the 1950's (Korean War); China at least until recently.

The best illustration of how our three factors: Canadian military prowess, the Indian Alliance, and American anti-Imperialism worked together to win a Canadian victory in 1812-14, is the Battle of Queenston Heights.

The Imperialist army went into battle already seriously weakened in numbers, yet still more numerous than its opponents. The New York Militia had been called up 'to defend the United States'. Crossing the Niagara, invading Canada, to them, did not come under that category. They stayed on the other side, their only role that of spectator.

Nevertheless, the Imperialists did manage to get sufficient forces across the river to attack the Canadian line. The Canadian line held.

Then the Mississauga Indians infiltrated the woods alongside the battlefields, climbed trees and began firing down on the bedeviled Yanks. Brock, a Canadian who had transferred his family and property to Canada, although already mortally wounded, ordered an advance. Then the Mississaugas came out of the woods, turned the retreat into a rout, killed many Americans and captured most of the rest. That particular Imperialist army ceased to exist as a fighting force.

Later in the war the Imperialists invaded Canada in overwhelming numbers — so overwhelming they defeated their purpose. They couldn't supply themselves and had to live off the land, loot, murder, and burn the houses of resisting civilians. Much of the Canadian population of the time was of recent American origin and not United Empire Loyalists either. Largely they had come to get away from the social chaos existing in the super-capitalist United States . . .

The war became a Peoples War, and from then on the American cause was hopeless.

PROSPECTS: THE INDIAN ALLIANCE

Canada owes its very existence to the Indian People. Unfortunately for the Indians — and almost everybody else — Canada is a bourgeois country, a colony in fact. Gratitude plays no part in bourgeois relationships.

The Indian Alliance was deliberately broken by the Canadian Comprador government as soon as the fur trade ceased to be of major importance. First, in the Red River Aggression against the Metis People. Then by a deliberate breaking up of all Indian governmental structures.

The Indian Alliance was smashed and it was done very cleverly, using the pretence that it was still valid. All this was completely unnecessary. The Indian People were quite ready to change their ways. In fact, the Plains Indian Culture was not ancient but modern, of more recent origin than Capitalism.

The appalling poverty in which more than half of Canada's Indians live has been so detailed it requires no comment here. The very way this poverty is stressed by know-nothing Liberals (including Indian ones) is racist. It gives the impression that Indians as a people cannot cope with modern conditions.

What are the Odds ?

Most *white* people can't really cope with modern conditions: this is a society planned, not for the people, but for the bourgeois. The fact is that, in spite of all the impositions laid upon them, many Indians do as well as can be expected. Many work as cowboys, long distance truck drivers, high steel workers — any job in which the boss is far away. They object to the extreme modern type of proletarian work-discipline, and in some of their own enterprises have shown it to be useless and unnecessary.

While our compradors have lost us the Indian Alliance, Canadian patriots can get it back. It can be done because it must be done.

It is ridiculous to say most of Canada is uninhabited. Most of Canada is inhabited by Indians.

The Ecology Movement must be treated as a vital part of the Anti-Imperialist struggle in Canada. To the Indian, especially the woods Indian, so vital to the continuation of Indian culture and identity, Ecology is a matter of life or death.

American tourists swarm over the north woods, shooting moose and deer. As bad as going into a farmer's pasture and slaughtering his cows. For a price, they can obtain the same 'aboriginal rights' for which Indians have to fight continuously.

All the schemes — the co-ordinated North American Water and Power Alliance (NAWAPA) to turn the North into a reservoir for hydro-electric power and the export of water to satisfy the diabetic thirst of the American industrial colossus — mean absolute ruin to the Indians.
There is not as much water as you would think, looking at a map. The many lakes and rivers that leak over the land are the result, not of plentiful water, but low evaporation and poor drainage. Think of the fire warnings and colossal fires every spring and summer. In fact, total precipitation in the North is very low. Lower than many deserts. At the height of summer, much of the tundra does become a desert. Canadian water is probably not a renewable resource at all. Like oil it could simply be drained away — and when it's gone it'll be gone.

NAWAPA (the James Bay scheme is only a part) would flood the beaver ponds. There goes the Indians' money. Moose and deer feed largely on water plants in the beaver ponds. There goes the Indians' food. In fact, in parts of the North, the Canadian Liberation struggle has already begun.

It is absolutely necessary that Canadian Patriots assign forces to work with the Indians, co-operating with them in this struggle. White leadership is probably out of the question, as Indians have good and understandable reasons to reject any sort of White leadership. The White and Indian struggles could be parallel, or Indians could be the leaders . . .

Effective co-operation with the Indian People depends in its turn on the enlistment of the Working Class . . . which is Canada's most patriotic class but as yet does not know where to turn. It has to be sure the Canadian Liberation struggle is primarily for its benefit — and for the benefit of all working people, including Indians.

It is the Indian's task to arouse themselves, and knowing what they do about the Yanks, knowing it better than we do, they may rouse themselves much quicker than you think. The case of the Indians doesn't correspond to the case of the Montagnards in Vietnam. Those Montagnards were a primitive people. The Indians are a modern people, using every tool and technique appropriate to their lives and their pocket books.

PROSPECTS: THE U.S. ANTI-IMPERIALISTS

The fact that a very significant part of the American people are anti-imperialists has not seemed to have worked so well in the Vietnam War. It is Vietnamese victories and not the American anti-imperialist movement which are bringing the end of that war into sight.

The movement was co-opted by middle-class elements who persisted in making it an anti-war rather than an anti-imperialist struggle. The stubborn facts are that war can be combatted only with war — plus other methods equally militant.

What are the Odds ?

Still the Black Panthers and some other groups have courageously condemned Imperialism, called for its overthrow, called for victory for all assaulted peoples of the world. When we think of possible war between the U.S. and Canada, a War of National Liberation, we mustn't be isolationist; mustn't forget that Yanks as well as Canucks are capable of thinking and analyzing previous mistakes.

Unlike the movement against the Vietnam War, which took years to gather steam, an Anti-Imperialist Movement inspired in the U.S. by a war against Canada could spring up in weeks. It would spring up as soon as Canadians showed themselves able and willing to defend themselves.

The most serious weakness of the 'Anti-War' Movement in the States was and is its failure to penetrate in any serious way into the proletariat. Here we've got to remember that many Americans are of Canadian birth or recent origin, and a rather large proportion of these are proletarians. Others have close family connections with people in Canada.

CANADIAN LIBERATION IS THE KEY

We stand a chance, a chance amounting to a certainty. The strategic and tactical problems of such a war would be immense — but not insurmountable. A people armed with a modern Marxist-Leninist ideology is invincible in a defensive war.

That problem requires an article at least as long as this, and need not be written by me. It is being discussed and taken seriously by more and more Canadians all the time.

I'm not guaranteeing the war would be short. I'm not predicting it'd be long. It could possibly be a series of short wars punctuated by and ended by revolutionary uprisings in the Heartland of Imperialism.

Patriotic Canadians must resolve to liberate themselves. Every nation has not only a right but a duty to be free. We are the principal colony of the American Empire and the key one. By consenting to be slaves, we injure every people struggling to be free. Deprived of its ownership of Canada, the principal Imperialist Power could never survive.

The Microscopic Army Ants of Corsica

The microscpic army ants of Corsica :
                                    It's the truth
                                    They exist
As surely as rhinoceri and elephants exist
And this poet exists to know
That each of them is definitely a creature as ever was
A specimen of Smilodon or Tyrannosaurus . . .

I know the liberals'ld quarrel with this
— carping on the word 'existence'.
"If a microscopic army ant were to fall from a tree
would it ever hit the ground? Would the impact be heard?"
I reject this liberal question along with the liberal assertion
"If you're not poverty-stricken you have no right to complain
                            AND
If you're poverty-stricken you've got no rights at all . . ."

Their ancestors had gotten isolated on an island
(it's explained by scientists after observation so close
that in their dreams they consulted with 'em)
And started getting smaller to fit that island
Like the reasoning power of a Ph.D.
When he's specialized and specialized down to the smallest
    specialization of his specialization
Til only one braincell is actIve, and that sleepily . . .
Perhaps (one theory happens to go)
The hunting got richer and richer as they got smaller
    and smaller
Til now they spend happy weeks in a rabbit's ear
Hunting fleas like cavemen after mammoths.

It's said that once when Napoleon was young and
    his head afflicted with lice
A great campaign was fought in his hair
So somehow he got onto the language
Listening to their tactical discussions . . .

Another story
Is that he was actually the reincarnation
Of a subaltern who if he had lived
Would've gone on to great things ——— the conquest of
    entire marijuana leaves
But died when one of the Bonapartes' feudal enemies
Cursed that family, grinding his teeth thereafter . . .

O Corsica! Hoary with battles
How glorious your great name was recognized
Before someone looked into a microscope and discovered
        its littlest corporal!
You who conquered the centre of Europe!
                                    How sad it was that
                                    the inhabitants after all
                        Turned out not to be lice but men
Stubborner in defeat than ever in victory

How sad it must have been for your most infamous son
To discover that Europe   —   even proportionately —
        was larger than his head
Contained more things than was contained in his head
And went on and on to places which in his head were
        represented by a void
But by themselves represented no void at all!

The microscopic army ants of Corsica
Have found themselves in impossible situations
(in the middle of a racetrack for instance
A roadless desert for them, afflicted by inexplicable
        solid hurricanes)
Whereupon they've organized bureaucracies, appointed
        commissions
To study the difficulty in great detail;
Filed reports, held debates, considered all established
        interests
Let the humble workers in to grouse all they liked :
Went on exactly as before til the whole people perished . . .

The microscopic army ants of Corsica
Have come to the shores of puddles — seas;
And since all experience has told them
Those seas eventually evaporate, just wait :

                The trouble
Happens, naturally, when they actually come to the shore
      of the sea;
Whereupon, as is the custom, they wait
Through an entire generation cometimes
Or a great wave comes and washes them away . . .
They've also considered the great social problem
of female supremacy —
              But the drones
              in their irrefutable majority

Among drones that is
Have insisted on their right to be sexual cymbols
Clang! Clang! Clang! Clang! Sexual cymbols!
Also their right to fly away! away! away!
To that incredible blue whitewash heaven
Where it's known all drones go when they fly

The microscopic army ants of Corsica
Have a problem; whenever they realize they have a problem
They start screaming about it
Til no sense can be heard :
That is they have a social group called 'liberals'
The name spelt with a big 'L' when the liberals are in power;
Who when they are out of power start to scream,
      scream, scream
Whenever they have a problem — scream that all is lost
Or at least that all is lost
Unless that problem — and that one only
Is considered . . .
           Once elected they do
Exactly as has been done before — NOTHING

All may be lost but at least the Liberals
Normal and righteous inheritors of the Earth
Are in power
        That's what counts

                        * * * * * * * * * * * * * * * * * * *

War—Bonnet

I wear the bonnet and I carry the lance.
I carry the shield which is my life
(not so much the shield as the design upon the shield;
not so much one design, as designs,
not so much designs as dreams
some of mine, some of other men, but all within
     the Tribe   —)

And I often wake lonely thinking "Why?"
(as I'd already been thinking in the dream)
Only within the tribe? Why not other tribes?
And would that give me extra strength or weakness?
I hurt at the thought . . . Why strength? Why weakness?
The answers seem too easy . . .
I cannot retreat : It is either/or
With me . . . The victory of Life or the victory of Death.
Some say I have killed with that lance. But I
Know it was the lance which killed   —   not me.

And I rode off not he . . .
But if he'd rode off my ghost would have watched him;
Watched him for my desire
That he should ride more splendidly than me

196(?)
23/8/70

On Regent Street and Elsewhere

Brother if your were dead I'd recount
After the style of a Canuck worker
Your deeds with glory and laughter
As a grizzly recalls old kills   —   escapes and escapades.

Or wear a button, curious, ambiguous
Saying nothing of it unless asked
Then tell of you along with other jokes
We humans play on circumstance and death.

But you're alive (at least exist
in some state reminiscent of life.
I don't quite get it. What's the idea?
A decent corpse would lie down

Ceasing to confuse   —   with loving memories   —   friends
Who know your history. I feel for them
But of you feel absolutely nothing. My main quarrel
With despair is that it's useless
And a luxury . . . not for our class.

First this was told me by enemies
Who of course rejoice : Including Trotskyites
To whom you give complacent shelter :
But oh my friends it's true. Stake your hearts elsewhere.

The bum in the street . . . He doesn't work
Which has a positive aspect.
He doesn't work for the American Empire.
The drug-peddlers posing as activists

Have some use. To maintain the act
They think they're fooling me with
Must tell sometimes, if not the truth, the facts.
Me? I'm a poet. Not a brain-surgeon.

The inward aspects of your decay
Interest me not at all. The outward aspects
   — they're the ones might interest me.
But I'm no Baudelaire. They interest me not at all.

Nothing's worse than a man gone sour with virtue.
He sits on that, his virtue, like a throne or a toilet;
First saying he must hold the position.
Then forgetting he ever said it.

Any live dog outroars a dead lion.
I shall sometimes hang around your vicinity
Cultivating peace and detachment about you
While looking for a likely batch of puppies.

A.M. May 10th
1972

Gentle Goddess

Gentle Goddess! Bride of the wounded!
No flame searches so deep as your white tongue's caressing

No moment sets itself inside itself as yours does
Last thing that moves in the delicacy of day . . .

Gentle Goddess! Gentle Goddess!
                              JEN
                                        TIL
                    GAW'
                                                  DESS!
How is it I call her gentle whom I saw last night
Among the fires of a city's noisy dying?
Her eyes came out in the spaces between various-colored
    plumes
Of smoke — plumes like the tails of giant felines
    waving over all . . .
They were like the moons of an alien planet;
And in each eye there was a wheel-shaped cage
In which little rodents ran or hesitated forever
Sometimes switching directions . . .

Gentle Goddess! Gentle Goddess!
                              JEN!
                    TIL!
                                        GAW'!
            DESS!
Lady I wish I was by nature permitted
To wish I was religious; and if I was a sniper
To wish every bullet inscribed with a prayer
That he not be hit but frightened narrowly;
That he be, in some mind-corner aware
I was right, and the clipped irregular suddenly ending
Song of the bullet shock him into qualitative growth . . .
Or wish for a wound, incapacitating only briefly;
Or failing all else, wish for a soul to pray for . . .

Grey-feathered soul, trembling like a bird in a cat's jaws :
No move of yours thru the decorated kingdoms
Hasn't had its contradiction . . .
                                    What I must wish
Is that in every turn I be honestly wrong or right,
That I question my honest civilization, my honest savagery,
And within the compass of certain honest necessities
I remain honest enough to change

Gentle Goddess! Bride of the wounded!
The wounded to death, to whom there's no time to say more;
And the wounded   —   the only wounded
Whether the wound be open or bacterial, of thoughtlessness
    or of the mind;
For all of these I hope to wish to pray
In your name, whether it be Birth or Death, Changelessness
    Change or the changelessness of continuing change;
That friend and enemy know you, that
When consciousness is fluttering like a moth, the heart
    likewise
They know you: And breathe themselves out with their thanks

19/7/70

Now follows the credit list . . .

Live with Me on Earth (in different versions)

The Canadian Forum
Made in Canada

What Right has He?   *The Square Deal*
The Garbageman is Drunk   *Katharsis*
In Ottawa   Streets   *Eldon Garnets Mag*

Ode to the Timothy Eaton Memorial Church

Made in Canada

Ho Chi Minh   *The Nationalist*
She . . .   *Made in Canada*
The Schooner Blue Boose   *New Canada*
Bethuniverse   *The Varsity*
Poem on Life Insurance and Combat Aviation

The Tamarack Review

Rabbie Still be with Us   *The Broadaxe*
The Mine is also of Nature   *This Magazine is about Schools*

NC PRESS LTD

publishes and distributes works of historical and social significance to Canadians today.

The History of Quebec—A Patriote's Handbook, by Léandre Bergeron	$1.50
The Prevention of World War III, by Harold Bronson	$2.75
The Trade Union Movement of Canada, 1827-1959, by Charles Lipton	$5.00
Why is Canada in Vietnam? Claire Culhane	$1.50
The History of Quebec: The French Regime. *In Pictures!* by Léandre Bergeron Robert Lavaill	$1.00

Books from Quebec

Petit manuel d'histoire du Québec, par Léandre Bergeron	$1.00
L'histoire du Québec, illustrée (le Régime Français)	$1.50
La conquête! par Léandre Bergeron and Robert Lavaill	$1.50
Les Boss du Québec — Les tigres de carton	$1.00
Les Boss du Québec — Les compagnies de finance	$1.00
Poèmes et chants de la résistance deux disques	$6.95

Books on National Liberation Struggle

On New Democracy, by Mao Tse Tung	$0.25
Lenin on the National Liberation Movement	$0.50
Quotations from Chairman Mao Tse Tung	$0.50
Selected Readings from the Works of Mao Tse Tung	$1.00
Imperialism, the Highest State of Capitalism, by Lenin	$0.50

Please send me:

. . . . . . copies of . . . .

. . . . . . copies of . . . .

. . . . . . copies of . . . .

Enclosed please find a cheque for $ . . . .

NAME . . . .

ADDRESS . . . .

CITY .ZONE . . . . .PROV . . . . .

A Complete list of books and music is available on request.
Please send prepaid mail orders to **NC Press Ltd., Box 6106, Terminal A, Toronto 1, Ontario.**

Canada is a colony. Our trade unions, our natural resources, our culture, our universities, and our industry—all are controlled from across the border, the longest undefended border in the world, which we "share" with the largest imperialist power in the world.

There are those who, seeing the extent of the colonialism, believe the battle to be lost. We do not see it that way.

We see people across the country rising up against U.S. imperialism: Workers struggling to forge militant, democratic Canadian unions, farmers fighting U.S. agribusiness, students opposing the takeover of the universities by increasing numbers of American professors.

To end our exploitation, to build a new Canada where the people hold the real power, we must unite patriotic and progressive Canadians in a fighting organization dedicated to the achievement of independence and socialism.

This is the aim of the Canadian Liberation Movement.

CANADIAN LIBERATION MOVEMENT

Box 41, Station 'E', Toronto 4, Ontario
Box 620, Station 'B', Ottawa, Ontario
Box 481, Thunder Bay 'F', Ontario
Box 784, Waterloo, Ontario
Box 1595, Guelph, Ontario
Box 6272, Station 'F', Hamilton, Ontario
Box 5256, Station 'B', Victoria, B.C.

- -

. . . . . I would like more information about CLM

. . . . . I would like to join CLM

Here is a donation to help CLM grow $ . . . .

Name . . . .

Address . . . .

City, ... Zone . . . . Prov . . . .